P9-CMX-492

Caviar Dreams,
TUNA FISH BUDGET

Caviar Dreams,
TUNA FISH BUDGET

MARGARET JOSEPHS

G
Gallery Books
NEW YORK LONDON TORONTO SYDNEY NEW DELHI

G

Gallery Books
An Imprint of Simon & Schuster, Inc.
1230 Avenue of the Americas
New York, NY 10020

Some names and identifying details have been changed.

First Gallery Books hardcover edition April 2021

GALLERY BOOKS and colophon are registered trademarks of Simon & Schuster, Inc.

For information about special discounts for bulk purchases, please contact Simon & Schuster Special Sales at 1-866-506-1949 or business@simonandschuster.com.

The Simon & Schuster Speakers Bureau can bring authors to your live event. For more information or to book an event, contact the Simon & Schuster Speakers Bureau at 1-866-248-3049 or visit our website at www.simonspeakers.com.

Interior design by Jaime Putorti

Manufactured in the United States of America

10 9 8 7 6 5 4 3 2 1

Library of Congress Cataloging-in-Publication Data

Names: Josephs, Margaret, author.
Title: Caviar dreams, tuna fish budget / Margaret Josephs.
Description: First Gallery Books hardcover edition. | New York : Gallery Books, 2021. |
Identifiers: LCCN 2020055489 (print) | LCCN 2020055490 (ebook) | ISBN 9781982172411 (hardcover) | ISBN 9781982172428 (trade paperback) | ISBN 9781982172435 (ebook)
Subjects: LCSH: Josephs, Margaret | Television personalities—United States—Biography. | Fashion designers—United States—Biography. | Women fashion designers—United States—Biography. | Real housewives of New Jersey (Television program)
Classification: LCC PN1992.4.J67 A3 2021 (print) | LCC PN1992.4.J67 (ebook) | DDC 791.4502/8092 [B]—dc23
LC record available at https://lccn.loc.gov/2020055489
LC ebook record available at https://lccn.loc.gov/2020055490

ISBN 978-1-9821-7241-1
ISBN 978-1-9821-7243-5 (ebook)

"When you cease to dream you cease to live."

—Malcolm Forbes

CONTENTS

Caviar Dreams,
TUNA FISH BUDGET

Chapter One

RAISED BY WOLVES

I entered this world already a mini adult, an old soul. Coming out of the birth canal, I told my mother, *Spread a little wider, you're screwing up my hair*. And boom, I was born.

In all seriousness, though, I never really had a childhood. I felt that I was put on this earth to protect my mother and just be her friend, rather than experience what it was like to be a little girl. Did I enjoy my life? Yes. When I think back on it, in a way, I was the center of everyone's universe—my mother's and my grandparents'. But I don't remember it being carefree.

I never ate enough and I was much too skinny, which was frowned upon in the Hungarian immigrant culture, where food was a luxury and a meaty girl was considered beautiful. Still, Marge Sr. would dress me to the nines, because looking pulled together was the most important thing to her—certainly more important than something like school. I was basically her best accessory, the perfect doll that you could mold into whatever you wanted it to be.

We would go to the pool in our matching bathing suits, just like a sex-kitten Barbie and her cute little sidekick. I thought she was so beautiful, but I also thought it was totally normal to parade around poolside, twinning with my mother in full weave, eyelashes, and high heels. I didn't realize till I was older, and in therapy, that this was *not* the norm. At the time, I wanted to grow up and be just like her. *Why wouldn't I? She got so much attention.* But I just wanted *her* attention.

I know she loved me, but she was young—only twenty when she had me—and by the time I was four years old, she would leave me crying at my grandparents' house because she was working or on a date. She would make excuses, and for some strange reason, I would have sympathy for her. *I* would be the one feeling guilty, which is not the way it should have been. It was some *Freaky Friday* role reversal.

But don't worry, I had a good way of making her feel badly too. I would bawl my eyes out, and then she'd buy me presents. I learned the art of manipulation at a very young age, which has worked well for me in life, so I guess her negligence served some purpose.

I didn't have a father to step in, which meant Marge Sr. didn't have anyone to share the burden of parenting with. My father, who was eleven years older than my mother, was Hungarian too. They were both FOBs—fresh off the boat. He was a handsome bad boy, right up my mother's alley. She was always attracted to men who didn't treat her nicely. And my father happened to fall into that category.

My mother didn't intend to get pregnant, but once it happened, she and my father decided to get hitched, in a romantic ceremony at the courthouse. She wore a brown-and-white polka-dot pantsuit. The outfit alone was an omen of things to come . . . Seriously, Marge Sr., what were you thinking? I doubt she would have married him if she hadn't been pregnant, especially if my grandfather had had anything to say about it. In fact, he told her not to do it, but she didn't listen. She got married anyway, and had me, the little Marge. Fortunately, even though Margaret is a very serious name for a child, it suited my sophisticated nature. And no, people, it's not narcissistic to name your daughter after yourself in Hungarian culture, though it does seem strange to most. I always answer any question about my insane life with *Hey, we're European*, and that shuts them up. You should try it next time you're at a loss for words.

I didn't know that having no father around was abnormal, even though all my friends had one. I thought it was optional, like small fries or large? Once I was a bit older, I remember saying to Marge Sr., *Mommy, where's my daddy?* And she answered, *He's not around. We're divorced*, which I took at face value, because you can't miss what you never had.

What I did not realize was that there was much more to the story.

Apparently, my father was both verbally and physically abusive to my mother (I didn't find that out until years later when I saw their divorce papers). She told me there was one Easter when she couldn't make it to my grandparents' house because he'd beaten her up so badly that she was in the hospital, and they had to lie about why my mother couldn't be there. My grandfather would have killed him for sure, and my mother saved him.

Thankfully, after a year and a half, she finally found the courage to file for divorce when I was about two years old. Then, Marge Sr., who's known for her dramatic behavior, decided to move us out one day while he was at work. Basically, she tricked him. She acted very sweet, and as soon as he'd left, she called a moving company and packed all of our stuff, and off we went. She'd already lined up another apartment for us in Edison, New Jersey.

Unfortunately, my father did not appreciate this quick getaway. He was a very jealous man, and it caused him to have a nervous breakdown. Within a few weeks after our heated departure, she was already dating . . . classic Marge Sr. No grass grew under her feet. One eventful night, she stuck me at my grandparents' house and went on a date, and my father, unbeknownst to her, had been following her and was sent into a fit of rage. Instead of taking their breakup in stride, he waited in the bushes by her apartment as she brought her unsuspecting date back. Then he casually attempted to shoot them through the window! *No biggie.* My father felt that if he couldn't have my mother, no one should. Mercifully, the bullet missed. Of course, the date got freaked out and ran away. (I don't know what made Marge Sr. more upset, that she lost her date or that she was shot at.) So she called the police and my father was carted off to jail. Then she went to visit him and agreed not to press charges, because, sure, why would she do that?! She's always had a soft spot for the crazy.

Following that psychotic episode, my father was rarely ever

seen, unless he was attached to a bar. My mother decided we should never see him again. Good job, Marge Sr.! We think he's dead now. Honestly, I've never bothered to look him up. With my luck, he'd need money, and I can't take one more person trying to mooch.

In my younger years, I spent a lot of time with my grandparents, even though my grandmother never spoke English, only Hungarian. My grandfather was fluent in both. They lived close by our apartment in Edison. What's strange is I remember that our rent was $350 a month. Why would I even know how much the fucking rent was? Because my mother told me. She told me *everything*. It was TMI. Marge Sr. was always TMI, and to this day, she still is. The apartment was a one-bedroom in a complex with a beautiful pool. She would let me stay in the bedroom with her and sleep in her bed, which I loved. I would sleep with her for many years, and to this day, when we travel, I still cuddle up with her. Remember, we are European.

I think I saw my grandparents every day. We were very, very close. Marge Sr.'s parents were nothing like her. They were immigrants who saved every penny they made. Conversely, my mother—also an immigrant—was a decadent spendthrift. She would take me shopping twice a year to a very fancy children's store called Pride and Joy and buy me a full wardrobe, because that's where she had always wanted to shop when she was a child. Marge Sr. was always a hard worker and a great earner, but she was better at spending. She made sure that I had everything she was deprived of. As a girl, I was adorned like the perfect little doll. We were two glamour-pusses walking down the street.

I do recall tumultuous fights between my mother and my grandmother, in Hungarian. All of which I understood. Believe it or not, The Marge didn't speak a word of English until kindergarten. My grandmother would call my mother a gypsy whore, and my grandfather would always defend my mother. She was his favorite child since their son (my uncle) had died at the age of nine being blown up by a hand grenade back in Hungary during World War II.

Eventually, I did go to nursery school, at least for a little while, but I did not like it one bit, and I didn't understand nap time at all. I was not a child who napped. I was a child who watched soap operas. I grew up glued to *General Hospital* and *All My Children* at a young age, with my grandmother. Susan Lucci's character, Erica Kane, was my idol. So when I was suddenly not allowed to watch soap operas because I had to go to nursery school, I was like, *I'm flying the coop! Get me the fuck out of here!* I cried so hard and told Marge Sr. that I absolutely couldn't stay there. I was like, *Who are these people? They're too childish for me!* I dropped out and went back to watching soap operas all day with my grandmother, and sometimes went with her to clean houses. We would go to her clients' homes and they were very kind to me. They would feed me fabulous lunches while my grandmother worked . . . *Sometimes* I would help. I enjoyed doing that more than going to nursery school, but with that being said, I haven't cleaned a toilet since. During my dropout years, I also spent time perfecting my driving skills. I remember sitting on my grandfather's lap, helping him drive his big Cadillac when I was only three years old. I mean, there weren't car seats then, and I was very coordinated.

By the time I got to kindergarten, the kids had matured a little and I deemed them acceptable for me to socialize with. Still, each day after school I would go to my grandparents' house because my mother had a full-time job. She worked at a company called Anchor Motor Freight, and she climbed her way up the ladder from secretary to accounting supervisor. Marge Sr. had an amazing work ethic, to the point of prioritizing it ahead of everything. Making money to support us and give me a better life was important to her—unfortunately . . . try explaining that to a five-year-old who only wanted her mommy. Luckily, I focused on my schoolwork and did everything for myself, since Marge Sr. was extremely preoccupied. I was good in school up until my later years, when I was a little bit of a fuck-around, but I was always smart enough that I could pull it together. Marge Sr. didn't care; she felt it was my responsibility.

For most of my time growing up, my mother had an amazing boyfriend, Wayne, whom I absolutely adored and am still close with. He really was a father figure to me, though he seemed jealous sometimes of my relationship with my mother and would compete with me. For example, we would play air hockey together, and he would always accuse me of cheating when I won. Most men are sore losers, I've found. Regardless, we were very close, and he was very loving and doting. Wayne was actually the mailman who delivered mail to Marge Sr.'s office, and she made sure she took advantage of the situation, since he got off work early. She would have him pick me up from school many days, and we would do my homework together and watch the Muppets. Wayne had issues with second-grade math, something to do with a new style of teaching . . . *Need I say more?*

Wayne also bought me my first dog, for which I am forever grateful. He still speaks of the dent it left in his bank account thanks to my mother, who insisted I have a purebred! We'd seen the cutest Lhasa apso at the park, and I'd fallen in love. My mother told Wayne in the nicest Marge Sr. way, "Margaret wants that dog. Go to the bank right now and take out the cash." I remember the dog costing a ridiculous amount of money. Probably close to $250, which was insanely expensive for the seventies. But poor Wayne would have done anything to please Marge Sr., so he did exactly as she said, on his mailman's salary. The next day we were at the breeder, cash in hand, bringing home my new puppy. From the minute she arrived home, she ruled the house. So we appropriately named her Queenie, therefore giving me the best stripper name (your first pet's name + the name of your first street = your stripper name). Hellooo Queenie MacGregor!

Marge Sr. had Wayne wrapped around her finger, and while she did love him very much, for some reason he was never enough for her. She felt that Wayne was not evolving and advancing, so she kept all her married boyfriends on the side. Looking back, I think Wayne wanted to marry her. Incidentally, I found out as an adult that Wayne was married to a woman named Judy when he met Marge Sr. But he left Judy a week after meeting my mom. So Marge Sr. really had the power of the puss! What's funny is that, years later, Wayne and my mother would go out with Judy and her new husband. Very civilized.

My mom and Wayne had a lot of friends, which I loved. Art and Dan, Danny and Cathy, Ronnie and Lisa—I remember all of their names because they had such an impact on my life. They were all so sweet to me. It was the swinging seventies and there was a lot of fun. I saw them partying and in various stages of undress. It was wild. I knew every intimate detail of their lives, like that Ronnie and Lisa were having affairs. Why I needed to be privy to information like that is beyond me, but at the time it made me feel special. I was getting the inside scoop; I was everyone's little BFF. I was loved and important. Years later in therapy I found out this was a big no-no and that it had given me my issues with feeling unsafe. Therapy taught me that I hadn't been old enough to process this adult information and that the privilege was actually more of a burden. Children need stability, not uncertainty. Ask Marge Sr. and she would say, *It was the Nixon years. Get over it.*

Marge Sr. was always ahead of her time socially. I recall seeing Art and Dan hold hands one evening at our house, and asking my mom where their wives were. She didn't bat an eyelash before responding, "Well, they are in love with each other." No big explanation necessary; it was completely normal. I never learned about the unfortunate discrimination the LGBTQ+ community faced until years later. It was shocking, and the reason I am passionate about being an ally to the community today. In Marge Sr.'s eyes, love is love, and that is what she taught me.

Marge Sr. had a lot of love to give, and though she loved Wayne she struggled to be faithful. Wayne knew my mother was unfaithful to him and he was always devastated. He would also confide in me as a young child. He'd say, "Your mother is crazy. She's difficult." I felt his pain. We would commiserate over Freihofer's cookies, which seemed to make everything better for the time being. Even now, I find myself reaching for cookies when Marge Sr. acts up.

The good news is that Marge Sr.'s men were always nice to me. They brought me extravagant gifts and were kind and loving. They knew the quickest way to Marge Sr. was through me. My mother made sure of it. She also made sure that I knew how to keep a secret. It was an unwritten rule: *Don't tell Wayne about the other men.* I'll never forget one night when some guy my mom was screwing around with was hiding in the closet. Wayne had just bought her a beautiful fur coat with much of his savings, and she decided to wear the fur coat on a date with someone else. Not surprisingly, Wayne found out, and before they left for their date, he came banging on the front door. The guy panicked and hid in the closet. I said to my mother, "I have to let Wayne in." And she said, "No way!" Then she called the police and had him carted off. I felt so sad. I was like, *How could you call the police on Wayne?* But she didn't care. She just left me with my babysitter, Jane, and went out to dinner. Marge Sr. was a real piece of work. Poor Wayne, newly released from jail, came over the next morning like nothing ever happened, and we all made our way to the Pancake House. *All My Children* had nothing on us!

By the time I was nine, we'd moved into a town house development, two doors down from a rabbi and his wife, who had the cutest sons, Rafi and Michael Crane. They were my very good friends; Rafi was my first crush, and they took me to temple. It was my earliest foray into Judaism, and I showed up in my best dress, to impress. It was the anniversary of Kristallnacht, which I knew nothing about. I listened intently as they recounted the atrocious event. That night was also the first time I learned about the Holocaust. I specifically remember Rabbi Crane talking about the children being torn from their parents and watching them die. I left temple with a newfound respect and understanding of Jewish history. It still resonates with me to this day. Marge Sr. was very into exposing me to every religion and culture.

At this time, I also convinced my mother that I no longer needed to go to my grandparents' house after school and that I could go home to our town house. I said I could take care of myself. And she was like, *Oh, you think so? Okay.* I mean, she took advice from a nine-year-old. Obviously, I was very convincing and she was very gullible. So we were the perfect pair.

Sidenote: I did still have to make a pit stop at my grandparents' sometimes, to administer my grandmother's insulin shot. A mini Nurse Ratched trying to not kill my grandmother with air in the syringe while also poking her a little extra hard on days she annoyed me. Sick shit.

Anyway, back at the town house . . . Shockingly, nothing bad ever happened. I had lots of friends, including my best friend Vena, who was the daughter of Indian doctors. She was great. Since my mother would come home late from work, they would feed me delicious Indian food. It was the most diverse, amazing neighborhood. And Vena's parents were so good to me.

I will admit that I knew my mom was different from my friends' moms. Often, they felt threatened by her. I knew this because they would interrogate me on my playdates with their pointed questions. *Oh, so your mother works? What does she do?* Even as a little girl you can tell when someone's being snide. She was successful. She supported herself. She didn't have a husband and she didn't need one. All the husbands adored her. She was the life of the party—a very dynamic, big personality, which some of the moms didn't appreciate. She was a very modern bon vivant in a conventional New Jersey town. Let's remember that divorce was not common, and single parenthood brought a lot of judgment. Not at all fair, but she didn't help the case by showing up braless and in hot pants. I'm still jealous of those perky boobs!

On the other hand, my friends adored Marge Sr. She was the fun mom. She would take me and my friends shopping for Barbies. We would have sleepovers and she would let us stay up late eating endless snacks. She'd leave us at home with my fabulously fun babysitter, Jane Herbert, who would entertain us with her guitar playing and singing. She was a real Jewish Joni Mitchell. I liked that aspect of my mother—she was decadent, indulgent, and made us feel special, even though she was never the mom to make sure everything was okay.

Did she know she was different? Not in the moment. I was the adult in the relationship, the responsible one. I was constantly nervous and anxious. I mean, she didn't even know when to take me to the doctor. One time I told her I had a sore throat—I didn't complain a lot, so it should have alerted her that something was really wrong. But not Marge Sr.! I wound up getting scarlet fever because my strep throat got so bad. I was very, very sick. She just asked, "Why didn't you tell me you were so sick?" I was like, *Hello?* So instead I became the best hypochondriac there ever was. I took this as a lesson to advocate for myself and read every single medical encyclopedia possible. Plus, with all my hours of *General Hospital*, I was basically a doctor anyway. Once my kids were in the picture, they were at the doctor's every week. For God's sake, even our dog still goes to the vet in the middle of the night monthly . . . We get simultaneous UTIs. Not sure which one of us has the Munchausen.

Marge Sr. was quite the opposite and still is today. Her health is the least of her concerns. Last time she was in the hospital with pneumonia, the height of her concern was how soon I could get to her with a Starbucks. I guess it's nice to know some things never change.

What was most important to her in my childhood was endless partying; there was a party almost every week. Strangers with barely any clothing. Definitely the smell of pot, which I didn't recognize at the time, but can now detect a mile away, and I still hate it on my clothes. It was all free love and seventies substances. Let's not forget they were all in their twenties, children raising a child, or a child raising these children.

I never felt very safe or protected. That's been a common theme in my life—never feeling like anybody worried about me first. It's the parent's job to take care of the child, no matter how old the child is. It was role reversal right from the beginning. I was left on my own. I was this skinny little blonde girl with my Coppertone tan and cutoff shorts. Thinking back, these memories freak me out because I was too sexy for a little girl; too in the know, with a sense of humor that was far too grown up. Marge Sr. didn't purposely want me to feel unsafe; she felt that knowledge was power. She didn't want secrets between us, just full disclosure. The part she didn't realize was that I was a child, and I could not handle adult information; it stole my innocence.

While it was a lot of fun and games to Marge Sr. and her partying friends, it seriously impacted the choices I made. I never wanted to feel out of control. As a result, I've never drank or used substances to feel good and enjoy myself. Obviously I've had a few drinks in my life, but that's it. I believe my mother was a total alcoholic, and that many people are and don't realize it. You don't have to drink every day to be one—it's the drinking as a coping mechanism or to feel comfortable in your own skin. When I had my son, it brought back so many childhood memories, I had to ask Marge Sr. to stop drinking. I told her she wouldn't be allowed near him if she didn't. It sounds drastic, but this was what I needed for myself and our relationship, and she did that for us. She also smoked when I was little, and I begged her to stop. I said, "I don't want you to die." So she quit. I give her credit for that. Truthfully, she thinks I'm a Debbie Downer, but she might be alone in that thought.

There are two occasions from my childhood that really impacted my view on alcohol to this day. The first was when we went to the Sharitskys' fiftieth wedding anniversary—they were close friends with my grandparents. I remember exactly what my mother was wearing that night. She had on a stunning brown dress with yellow flowers; it was a halter and cut on the bias. She had a beautiful wig on, and my grandmother was so proud of how gorgeous she looked. We always were a shallow crew. My grandmother was a four-foot-eleven beautiful troll with an eye for the glam. I was little, but I also recall being happy that Marge Sr. was so pretty. This was my first out-of-the-house glamorous party at a country club. I felt like Cinderella in my white tulle dress. I was six years old and ready to dance the night away. We walked into the party with Wayne, and all eyes were on my mother. Wayne always felt that he had gotten the prize and everyone was trying to steal it—unfortunately, it was available for the taking. Marge Sr. instantly started drinking and flirting with another man. Not surprisingly, Wayne was jealous. I could just feel the uncomfortable energy.

There was a band, and I was dancing with my grandfather, but there was no denying that Marge Sr. was drunk, drunk, drunk, and throwing herself at this guy. I went over and said, "Mommy, stop. Please stop." She was laughing so hard that she almost fell over the balcony railing before someone grabbed her. At that moment, I broke out into a hysteria of cries and insisted on leaving. I couldn't stay and watch her self-destruct, so my grandparents took me to their house to sleep over. My mother didn't even know I was missing. Hello?!

The next morning, when she came to pick me up, I refused to go home with her. She was so fucking hungover. Her behavior stuck in my head and really disturbed me. I saw it had upset Wayne and my grandparents as well. Everything about it was ugly and not how I wanted to be. It was a confusing dichotomy to want to emulate her and to possess a distaste for her at the same time. On the one hand, I thought she was the most striking woman in the world. She was loving, affectionate, and attentive. She was also very smart and had an amazing work ethic; that's where I got it from. But on the other hand, I was repulsed by the drinking and the inappropriate actions that came with it.

The other event that I can recall, which started out really fun, was when Marge Sr. had all of her friends at our house and invited all the neighbors too. But when she figured out that my best friend Vena's parents and the other doctors in our town house complex were having a huge party of their own and weren't coming to hers, she decided to crash theirs instead. Marge Sr. dragged all of her guests over to Vena's house. My mother's friends couldn't take the spicy food, so she tried convincing all the doctors to go skinny-dipping in the community pool to "cool off." I think they were horrified that my mom and her crew were completely naked. I thought it was so hysterical.

Until the following day. I slept at Vena's house that night and overheard her parents talking about how crazy my mother was. And when I went home the next morning, everybody was half-naked and strewn across the living room, and there were dirty dishes piled up to the ceiling. I immediately called my grandparents to tattle on my mother. That pissed her off. *No one likes a tattletale, Margaret.* She didn't think she should have to answer to anybody, but I felt differently. I knew she wasn't a normal mom and was kind of a hot mess, emphasis on the word *hot.* While her appearance was always spotless and meticulous, she would rather have moved than clean the house. And therefore, I am meticulous and spotless with that too. Never one to use the same towel twice, I obsessively do laundry and dry cleaning.

Don't get me wrong, there are some elements of my formative years I can laugh about. Like when my mother signed me up for swimming lessons. Marge Sr. never learned to swim. She still can't swim. So it was very important to her that I learn. Of course she would show up in her bikini like a sex kitten and sit on the side of the pool to show off for the lifeguards and the male instructor. They just threw me in the pool. And while I was about to fucking drown, instead of paying attention to me, they'd be flirting with her. I'm not kidding. I was literally swallowing water and no one gave a shit. I immediately requested to switch to a female teacher so I didn't die. Amazingly, I became a great swimmer.

Humor aside, though, if I'm being honest, I don't really know what it's like to have a mother. I've never had one. I've said that to her, and I truly believe it. It definitely makes me sad. I know what I'm missing. I love her very much, but I still don't have that relationship with her. We're close, inseparable. Everybody knows that. We have a special relationship, but it's based on friendship, not parenting. I will say, to her credit, that everything she didn't give to me, she's given to my son. She's the ultimate grandmother. She has stepped up tenfold.

Life Lessons

- You can't choose your start in life, but you can choose how it impacts your decisions later down the road.
- The earlier you realize that you have to advocate for yourself, the better.

Chapter Two

SPEND YOUR LAST DOLLAR ON A LIPSTICK

Growing up, I had a very refined palate. Marge Sr. loved to feed me the breakfast of champions—coffee and Oreos.

When I started kindergarten, I was especially proud to share this information. All the kids sat in a circle, and everybody went around to say what they'd had for breakfast that day. One little girl had enjoyed pancakes (how basic). Others had indulged in eggs and bacon. But as soon as our teacher, Ms. Dietrich, came to me and said, "Margaret, what did you have?" I proudly announced my glamorous breakfast of coffee and Oreos. Immediately, I saw the horror on her face. She said, "Coffee and Oreo cookies? Well, that's not very healthy." Of course I was totally mortified. Until she got to Rudolph, who admitted he'd eaten hot dogs, which was much worse in her opinion, so I felt better about myself. Thanks, Rudolph.

But, you know, coffee kept me nice and perky. I mean, maybe that's why nap time really didn't work for me. I always loved my dose of caffeine. Then I went home and told Marge Sr., and she was like, "It's not a big deal. We're very European." That was always her answer to everything. *We're European.* European kids always drink coffee. I told my mother that I felt really badly that Ms. Dietrich was upset. She could see I was distressed. So for Christmas Marge Sr. bought her the most expensive perfume, which, at the time, was Estée Lauder Youth-Dew. The Oreos became a nonissue. If there was one thing my mother taught me very early in life, it was the art of the bribe. She knew that beautiful gifts put people in the right frame of mind, mainly when she'd fucked something up. I would say I'm the same way. I like to give beautiful gifts, but not because I fucked up. It's the old *You can catch more flies with honey* trick, and it works well.

My mother let me do whatever I wanted. I called the shots. Thus the coffee and Oreos. Though, in my defense, there wasn't much else to eat. Our refrigerator was like that of a bachelor. There were high-end cheeses, nuts, party snacks, and alcohol. Nothing else. That's how I kept my slim little figure. I think I weighed forty-eight pounds until I was in seventh grade. I looked like a stick figure—it was amazing. Everybody was always saying, *You're so skinny, you're too skinny.* I wish I was still so fucking skinny. Thank God for my grandparents or I might have starved to death. They made all my snacks and my lunches. But I never fully ate them. I would go to my grandparents' after school, and they would feed me again. That is, until I convinced my mother at age nine that I could fend for myself. Then I would make my own lunch of grilled cheese sandwiches.

The only time that Marge Sr. would offer sustenance of any kind was every Saturday. She and Wayne would take me to the Pancake House, and I would get the Rooty Tooty Fresh 'N Fruity. My mother would have her oversized sunglasses on because, now that I think of it, she must have been hungover. Back then I didn't realize it, but I do remember that she always needed coffee immediately and would have a hemorrhage if the waitress spilled any over the side of the cup. That would send me into a panic, because I thought Marge Sr. seemed like a wicked bitch with her sunglasses and big wig. I mean, she'd go in looking like a fucking movie star, with me, her skinny mini, and Wayne, with his leather jacket and mullet, following right behind her.

Marge Sr.'s priorities changed on a daily basis, based on whatever mood she woke up in. She preferred to buy me an entire new wardrobe than do laundry. Why have old when you can have new?! Sometimes the electricity would be shut off. God knows she'd likely spent our electricity funds on shoes, Diane von Furstenberg dresses, or a new fur. Honestly, Marge Sr. never worried about money, or if she did, she never showed it. I got everything I wanted, because she would completely live for the moment and worry about it never. I'm not like that. I buy, but within reason. And when I have to buckle down, I buckle down. When I don't have to, I don't. But my mother had an innate talent for compartmentalizing things and not concerning herself with what tomorrow might look like. She also assumed my grandparents would be there to bail her out if the shit really hit the fan. Listen, they weren't the Rockefellers, but they were hard workers and saved every penny.

Like the time Marge Sr. decided I was going to learn to play the piano. She'd never had the opportunity to take lessons as a child, so she went out and bought me the biggest and fanciest piano she could find. But it wasn't really for me. I'd never even mentioned an interest in it. She thought I had beautiful long fingers, which I don't—just long compared to her stubs. She wanted me to be the female Liberace. Everything she never had as a child, she wanted me to have. She lived vicariously through me. Her way of giving me attention was to shower me with everything she thought I wanted, but all I wanted was stability.

It was a very weird dynamic. I mothered her more than she mothered me. I was a neurotic wreck throughout my whole childhood. I didn't act nervous, but I was. I had a very mature attitude, and I knew way too much as a young girl, too many adult things. For example, I saw *The Exorcist* at the ripe age of six. Marge Sr. thought I would simply sleep through the movie, but I still have nightmares about it to this day. I still see Linda Blair's Regan coming out of my basement, with the green vomit spewing from her mouth, which absolutely freaks me out.

In the middle of the night I'd wake up and my mother would be repainting the entire house and redecorating. I was like, *Can this wait till morning??* And she'd reply nonchalantly, *I needed to change the color of the walls. Puce is in this season.* Of course that made complete sense. Being in style is still one of our core values.

Marge Sr. always had an explanation for her odd behavior. Most of the time, she blamed it on the diet pills she took (aka speed). She *was* always on a diet; that part was true. Even though all she cared about was how she looked, she didn't treat her body very well. Marge Sr. was always a fan of the fast fix. Why do an aerobics class when you could pop a pill? Why clean the house when you could move? Big on the solution, not necessarily the consequences. As I've said before, she was also big on the oversharing.

In fact, she once had a hemorrhage of her uterus while she was at work. And of course she told me all about it. She said, "I hemorrhaged and almost bled to death." Why would she tell me that?! I just pictured the inside of a cow on the floor and almost had a fucking nervous breakdown. I was constantly worried that she was going to die. Then I'd be stuck with my grandparents forever.

Not that I didn't love my grandparents, but they were much older and very conservative. The thought of being stuck at home all day watching soap operas, my only escape cleaning other people's houses—not the life for me. The not-so-funny thing is that my grandmother felt the same way. She'd say to me, "Your mother's going to die." I was like, *Fuck, I* am *going to be cleaning shit out of other people's toilets.*

I don't want you to think that Marge Sr. couldn't be a mama bear when necessary, especially when someone messed with me. *That* she did not like. No one wants someone screwing with their sidekick. So when one of the nuns at my Hungarian grammar school, Our Lady of Hungary, yanked me by the pigtails because I was running down the hallway, my mother was pissed. I didn't want to go back there. The next day Marge Sr. stormed into the school with her leather trench coat and big sunglasses and told Sister Emmerencia, the four-foot, two-inch bitch-on-a-Bible, in no uncertain terms, that she better not touch her daughter's precious pigtails ever again. Obviously, having my hair pulled is a pattern. Thanks, Danielle.

Not that the hair pulling was worth it, but it was a fast track to getting my mother's attention. I used to ask her why she couldn't stay home like my friends' moms. And she'd explain that she had to work in order to support us. Truthfully, I don't think she would have left her job even if we'd had all the money in the world. While she loved me, she preferred little kids, mainly infants—she was drawn to them. So as I got older, I felt like I aged out. I remember that she would pay attention to random little babies and I would get jealous. I was like, "What about me? What happened to me? Why aren't you paying attention to me?" And she'd say, "Stop it, you're so spoiled."

I think she probably would have wanted another child, but I don't think she could have handled having more. At some point I found out that when I was around seven years old, she'd had an abortion when she was with Wayne. She said, "You would have had a little brother or sister, but Wayne told me to get an abortion." Of course she had to fucking tell me that. I mean, why don't you stick another knife in, because every child should know their mother had an abortion. *We're very European.*

It's funny, because Wayne, whom I'm so close to, to this day, still thinks my mother is the greatest. He sees her through rose-colored glasses. He's always saying things like, *Your mother is the best. She loved you so much. I was envious when she would say Margie comes first.* And I'm like, *Wait just a minute. I love Marge Sr., but you have to see her for who she is. You can say whatever you want. But she did have you arrested on the front lawn.*

My mother and Wayne are still friends too, but I'm much closer with him than she is. He's married now, and his wife is great, but he will always say my mother is the love of his life. He never had children, so he considers me his daughter. I consider him my father as well. Unfortunately, we were physically separated for a little while when he moved to Florida with health concerns. We've had our ups and downs, only pertaining to his relationship with my mother. Doesn't every woman leave her single, fabulous boyfriend for an asshole with another family?

This may seem surprising, but the glamorous, successful sex kitten also known as my mother had very low self-esteem. I learned a lot about what *not* to do from her. It could have gone in either direction. I could have ended up totally like Marge Sr., always crying about some married boyfriend while neglecting the great single guys. Marge Sr. was very strong in business, but she was very weak for men. And I always swore to myself, *I'm not going to fucking do that. This isn't going to be my life.* I recognized that at a young age.

I did succumb to it a little bit with Jan, but not in the same way my mother did with her men. For one, I was married to Jan. And he was a great guy and a great father. My priority was to have a much different life with him than my mother had experienced in her relationships. But there are certain things I put up with that I'm not proud of. When I saw myself doing those things, I knew that my marriage wasn't right. We tried to go to therapy, even though it didn't work. My mother never would have done that, and she really could have benefited from it. She didn't know how to truly work on herself. Retail therapy doesn't count.

I think the reason I came out so secure is because I knew through it all that she loved me. Every day she told me a thousand times that she loved me. She would hug and kiss me constantly. Feeling truly loved makes up for a lot of crazy.

So I did feel adored. If she upset me, she was always apologetic and begging for forgiveness. It put me in a weird position of power over her, which was uncomfortable. But I got over it, because she would indulge me to no end.

We would go on these tremendous shopping sprees together. As I mentioned, she was obsessed with this store Pride and Joy, and we had to go there twice a year. It was in Perth Amboy, New Jersey, on Smith Street. My mother told me that when she was younger, she always dreamed that she would buy everything for her daughter from there.

The saleswomen at Pride and Joy would literally wait for us to walk in and then roll out the proverbial red carpet. We would go into this tremendous dressing room, lined in velvet, and my mother and I would sit there while they wheeled in racks of clothing. I would say *yay* or *nay* to whatever I liked and didn't like. It was very *Pretty Woman* of me.

This was something I looked forward to doing with my mother. I don't even know how much she spent, but those saleswomen saw dollar signs when Marge Sr. sauntered in. I got whatever I wanted. I'll never forget these amazing velvet pants she bought me. They were the perfect shade of green to bring out the color of my eyes. I knew how to work the system; I would try on fully accessorized outfits that were so fabulous Marge Sr. would just *have* to buy it all. It was completely over the top.

With a fully stocked new wardrobe, we would go out on the town for dinner with her boyfriends. Marge Sr. would braid my hair, put lip gloss on me, and treat me to a manicure. It was my thing with my mom. We had a lot of things, actually. Sure, she would sleep through my cartoons on Saturday morning, but it was our ritual for me to sit in her bed while she was sleeping and eat a bowl of Lucky Charms, which are still my favorite to this day—I pick out all the marshmallows and eat them first. I'd also make myself a cup of coffee, because what did she care if I stunted my growth? I think that's a myth anyway. I'm taller than she is and obviously not very stunted. In classic European fashion, my mother always slept in the nude. She passed that down to me—I'm not one to pack pajamas on a trip. She used to say, *Let's not be uptight about our bodies. We're Hungarian.* That pisses my Joe off. He's like, *We're in America! Stop running around naked in front of the windows!*

Joe knows that Marge Sr. marches to the beat of her own drum, but it's hard for anyone to really understand what it was like to grow up as her child. For example, there was the time she took me to the dentist, Dr. Silverman, and allowed him to smoke a cigarette while he was cleaning my teeth. Now, any normal person would be like, *Please don't smoke near my daughter*. But my mother was in her own world, flirting with Dr. Silverman. All was good until the fucking loser dropped ashes on my face and burned me. That got Marge Sr.'s attention. It was fine for him to give me lung cancer. But as soon as he damaged my beautiful little *punim*, my mother said, "Out of the chair, Marge, we're leaving." It was nice to know even she had her limits.

When I was in sixth grade, my mother got a job transfer and we had to move to Mahopac, New York. I felt very sick that we were leaving my grandparents behind. And I hated abandoning all of my friends. But Marge Sr. swore that Mahopac would be a better life for us. We got a big house with a big yard on an acre of land in Lake MacGregor, and she said it was going to be fabulous.

The truth is, we probably should have picked someplace closer to her job in Tarrytown, but Mahopac was less expensive and she wanted to save the extra $10,000 on a house, which was fine with me because I ended up loving it there.

I could have gone to a great private school in Tarrytown, the Hackley School, but after years of Catholic school I was ready for a change, and since I called the shots, off to public school it was. She never put her foot down when it came to me. She didn't understand that you don't let the child make the decisions. But hey, I was her best friend, not her child.

The other thing she did that, in my opinion, wasn't very smart was to leave Wayne in New Jersey. In the beginning, he would come up on the weekends, but Marge Sr. already had her married Hungarian boyfriend, Joe (he was also an FOB—and an SOB). The sick thing is that he was my best friend's godfather, and Marge Sr. met him at a party at her house. I saw my mother flirting with him right in front of his wife. Next thing you know, Joe was at my front door when we still lived in New Jersey. He said, "Oh, I was just stopping by on my way home from work to see your mother." I was like, *Really? You live in fucking Brooklyn!* He told me he had a job out here. *Because there's a major shortage of commercial plumbers in New Jersey, so we have to import them from Brooklyn, right?* That's how their affair started. He was very taken with my mother.

For years, their relationship continued in Mahopac. Joe was chauvinistic and extremely jealous of everything my mother did. He really did a number on her. And she allowed it. Probably because, when it first started, he was very generous. He bought her cars and gave her money. All the bullshit. But he was never leaving the wife. I'm assuming the wife probably knew about the affair. She had to, because he was never home. I don't even know how this guy managed to come to our house every single day, every single night, and all day Saturday when he had three kids of his own.

He was a total game player and obsessed with my mother. If he even had an inkling of any other men being interested in her, he'd go mental, screaming that she was a cheater. What's worse is that he tried to be parental to me, since my mother wasn't. But I was like, *Who the fuck are you coming into our situation? You have no say over me. You're not my father. You're not married to my mother, and you have a whole other family.* He always had too much to say and he wasn't pleasant about it. Thank God, years later, he died a horrible death from lung cancer. By the way, I'm not a bitch, but he really did deserve it.

Joe aside, I was happy in Mahopac. I had a lot of new friends, including one of my best friends in the whole world, whom I'm still very close with, Katie McMahon. She lived down the block. Her mother loves to tell the story about when we first moved there and I went to their house. We lived on the lake and my bathing suits weren't unpacked yet. Katie generously offered to loan me a suit so we could go swimming. So Katie's mother handed me a one-piece and I said, "Oh no, no, I only wear bikinis." Katie's mom was taken aback for a second until she heard the next line out of my mouth, which really sealed the deal: "Are there any boys around here? I just love boys." I mean, what eleven-year-old doesn't? She nervously laughed it off and handed me the only bikini Katie owned. I mean, there *were* boys to impress at the lake.

Katie's mother befriended Marge Sr., while the rest of the moms shunned her. It was very much like *Hide your husbands!* They were like, *Who is this new woman who's* divorced? Divorce was a big scarlet letter then. I felt like we had a *D* emblazoned on our front lawn. At first, the neighbors across the street wouldn't let me have sleepovers with their kids because of it. How fucked up is that? But never mind them, it was an open invite for sleepovers at Katie's house. There was a lot of that kind of behavior. I guess some women are threatened by confident single women. They didn't want Marge Sr. near their husbands. I'm not sure I can blame them for that . . . based on her history.

As I got older—fourteen—I had a lot of boyfriends. I had guys who were eighteen showing up on motorcycles to go out with me. There was one in particular named Paul who was just gorgeous. His face was so chiseled, with an amazing jawline framed by his long, thick hair and the most beautiful smile. Of course, he was of legal drinking age, so my mother would invite him in for a cocktail. She was thirty-four and flirting with *my* boyfriends.

They'd love talking to my mother. What's better than a mother-daughter duo? Even though, at this point, Marge Sr. *was* starting to pack on a few pounds, she still looked good. Either way, I didn't appreciate her presence. I was like, *Leave the room. It's so awkward.* But she loved any male attention, even if it was from *my* boyfriends.

When I was fifteen, I had sex for the first time with my first serious boyfriend, Chris—whom I'm still friends with to this day. When Marge Sr. found out (by reading my diary), she had a total hissy fit. There was no thoughtful discussion about how I should be careful, or any concern on her part about how I was feeling after the fact. That would have been too normal. Instead, she cried and, essentially, had a tantrum. Then her married boyfriend, Joe, had the nerve to say to me, "You upset your mother."

I upset my mother?! You're fucking your wife and Marge Sr. at the same time! Like I'm going to listen to you! I mean, seriously. But at the time I was fearful, because I'd disappointed them. Can you believe I was worried about disappointing some married freak? All of it was very hypocritical. I didn't see it then, but I knew something was off. Did it stop me from having sex with Chris? Absolutely not. I was having the time of my life.

Most young girls were not happy with their first sexual experience. Mine happened to be completely fabulous. Chris came from an amazing family, and they were all very warm and nurturing to me. His older sister, Judy, is one of my best friends and was the maid of honor in my wedding to Jan. Every day after school I would go home with Chris, because there was never any food in our house, and his mother would make me a delicious sandwich of cream cheese and tomatoes on Italian bread. Then we would have sex in his bed—*don't worry, his mother never left the kitchen*. I'd be so exhausted after that I'd have to take a nap on the sofa. He was such a neat freak that he would vacuum around me while I was sleeping. Once I was fully rested, we'd do our homework together before my mother picked me up. We couldn't get enough of each other. It was the perfect relationship—great sex, good food, and he cleaned while I slept. Much like my life today. Chris and I rendezvoused on and off until I met Jan. We truly could never have spent a life together. I would have driven him absolutely insane. Let's just say my spontaneity and, as I like to call it, joie de vivre are not for everyone . . . It's fun for a good time but not a lifetime, unless you're Joe Benigno.

I would have huge parties at my house—fifty to sixty kids would come over on a Friday night. We'd play RCK (run, catch, and kiss) and spin the bottle. We'd make little campfires in the backyard and my mother would let all the girls and boys sleep over in tents. She was very fun that way. I mean, did she watch us? Nope. God knows what the fuck was going on. We could have been eaten by a bear, and she wouldn't have known until the next morning.

Recently, at a Christmas party, Judy reminded me of one famous story. She remembers coming over to my house, and my mother, whom Judy calls Big Marge, answered the door wearing a negligee with marabou slippers. This was a typical outfit for Marge Sr. later in the day. Totally appropriate attire for a madam, which she was obviously channeling most days. Anyway, my mother greets Judy and invites her in for a cocktail. Of course, when Judy recounts it, she gives my mother a heavy Hungarian accent, like she was Eva Gabor from *Green Acres*. And Judy is like, *No thank you, I'm just coming to pick up Chris and Margaret.* And my mother insists that Judy should stay and have a drink, even though Judy tells her that she's just gotten her license and she has to drive, for Christ's sake! So what does Marge Sr. say to this? "Don't be silly; one drink won't hurt you."

Now, listen, I get that in retrospect it seems like something to laugh about, but when Judy shared it with everyone at this huge Christmas bash, my mother looked at me and she was horrified. Joe looked at me and he was horrified. I was horrified too. Because the three of us knew everything that was going through my mind. We got in the car and I said, "Do you fucking see what I have to deal with?" Marge Sr. started crying. I started crying. Joe started mimicking us, and was like, *Girls, girls, calm down*. He knew how to turn our tears into laughter.

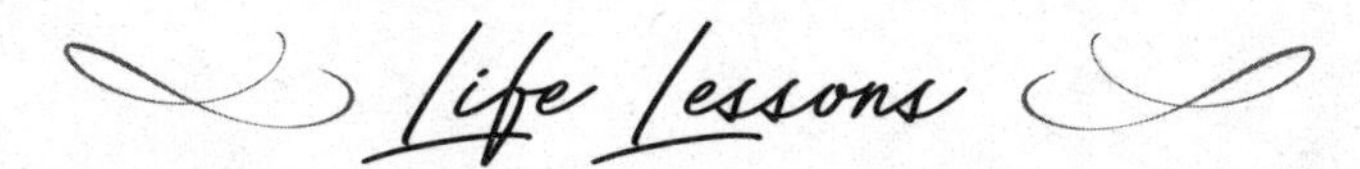

- When you have children, remember that you are their parent first before being their friend.
- In adulthood, knowledge is power. In childhood, there's a fine line before it's a loss of innocence.

Chapter Three

LEADER OF THE PACK

I was one of those girls who was sent home from school for not wearing any underwear. I'm not sure how the principal figured that one out—I guess he saw me standing in the light wearing my long, white Norma Kamali dress, or at least I hope that's what it was. Of course, I was the only student at Mahopac High who even knew who Norma Kamali was. I actually found the whole thing completely entertaining—my mother, not so much.

It was sort of arbitrary what bothered her and what didn't. I mean, getting caught with no underwear was unacceptable, but it was perfectly fine for our oil tanks to run dry, so that we had no heat on the coldest days of winter. Or for us to run out of food (for both us and the dogs). Not to mention the spoiled milk in the refrigerator. But we never ran out of face cream and lipstick!

Marge Sr. was someone who probably shouldn't have lived in a house. She should have found a full-service apartment building instead. But that didn't suit her fly-by-night nature. She loved the ability to obsess over something and have it take over our space. Like when she went on a plant kick and bought thirty-five of them. It was like living in a jungle. Or when, on the spur of the moment, she'd decide to redo the bathroom. We'd go to Bloomingdale's and purchase twenty-five new towels, rugs, and accessories. Everything was in excess. Nothing in moderation.

Our bathroom was like a makeup store. We had every eye shadow, every color lipstick, every type of hair product, every blow-dryer, and about twenty-five curling irons. The more glam, the better. We walked out of that house looking like two strippers from Las Vegas.

Of course, every good stripper needs a waterbed, right? And Katie McMahon had one, so I had to have one too. I told Marge Sr., and she said, "Of course, sweetheart." I don't think it's necessarily appropriate for a teenage girl to have a heated, king-size waterbed to bang her boyfriend on. But hey, it was a lot of fun and it made for some good times. A little motion in the ocean.

New Year's Eve: the culmination of my mother's life of excess. My mother would take about ten of us, including my boyfriend, Chris, and his entire family, to The Manor in West Orange, New Jersey, and spare no expense. I guess it brought back memories of her first date with Wayne, when she lovingly vomited all over his brown polyester suit. Wayne thought he was getting lucky with Marge Sr. after her two gin martinis; he didn't realize the only luck he was getting was two orders of lobster thermidor. Or the times the three of us—my mom, Wayne, and I—would sneak into weddings there and pretend we were guests. We were the original wedding crashers. I would dance with the father of the bride and Marge Sr. would catch the crystals falling off the chandeliers as souvenirs and stuff them in her purse. We were real class acts.

But back to New Year's Eve . . . It was our fashion event of the year. We would all get dressed to the nines to glamorously dance the night away in West Orange. Since it was the year's end, Marge Sr. would cry and thank everybody, and say how grateful she was. It was her way of giving back to everyone who'd done things for her that year, and everyone she'd neglected. The resolutions would stick for a good five days, and then we'd have another 360 to think of new ones. The Manor is still a constant in our lives. When my son was young, Marge Sr. would bring him there for dinner dates every weekend, and we still go for special occasions.

In my opinion I was old enough to take care of myself at age nine, so by the time I was a teenager I really was on my own. When Marge Sr. wasn't working, she was typically sleeping from the exhaustion of fighting with her married boyfriend or having sex and cocktails all afternoon, which in hindsight doesn't sound so terrible. This meant that it was very easy for me to sneak out of the house. I would steal one of Marge Sr.'s outfits, because she was still thin enough, and then her car. I would put it in reverse to roll it down the driveway and then start the engine when it was out of earshot. Then I'd go pick up Katie, who by now I had nicknamed Stubs (she was short and petite; I think it's self-explanatory), and we would haul our hot asses into New York City.

I'll never forget one of the times we went to the Limelight. Stubs and I had on these amazing dresses with lace gloves. We stood outside with every other wannabe and waited for the bouncer to peruse the crowd to pick his favorites to go in. Stubs and I were at the top of the list. Young and nubile were ideal qualifications for such a debaucherously fun club. I wish it was still open today.

We danced all night with random men, and Stubs ended up meeting the cutest guy. His name was Chris D'Andretti, and she was like, *I want to leave with him*. I mean, we were going home with complete strangers from the fucking Limelight at sixteen years old. It was sick. I miss those days when your only worry was getting pregnant or VD, both curable.

So we went back to Chris D'Andretti's apartment on the Upper East Side so Stubs could have sex with him. Chris was short and sweet and hard to beat. Very cute. He lived with his brother, Matt, who was about six-foot-three and extremely handsome. Matt was like, *Who are these girls?* And I was like, *Who's this gorgeous guy?* I thought, *Wow, city boys on the Upper East Side are fabulous. This could be our new life!* I decided to curl up in Matt's bed with him, even though—believe it or not—we did not have sex.

Unfortunately, Katie freaked out and ran into Matt's bedroom to tell me she didn't want to stay over. She said Chris's dick was so big, like a birth defect, and she didn't want to have sex with him again. I was like, *Oh my God, that's horrible! Did it hit your tonsils?* So we had to skedaddle out of there. On our way home, I got in a car accident. I rear-ended someone on the FDR Drive, and Stubs's head hit the window. I was like, *Holy shit, now she cracked my windshield with her hard head.*

The people I'd hit were this very nice Spanish family, and they were screaming hysterically. I said, "Listen, my mother is going to kill me. I can't wait for the police. The only damage is on my car." I only had a junior license and wasn't supposed to be driving in NYC. We really just hightailed it out of there. Stubs had a welt on her head, which was horrible, but I was like, *Your head? We could have been thrown in jail, get over it.* I was always very sympathetic. We drove home to my house, snuck inside, got undressed, and slipped into my waterbed like nothing had ever happened. My mother never caught us; I told her a tree branch must have fallen on the car.

Before we were sneaking into clubs, Stubs and I would spend our Fridays and Saturdays at the roller rink. We would roll up, literally, in our rabbit-fur coats and satin Sassons, which were so skin-tight we'd have to close the zippers using pliers. We'd skate double sessions, from four in the afternoon to eleven at night. No wonder I was so fucking skinny. We'd close out the rink, slip on our high-heeled Candie's in the dead of winter, and click across the parking lot to McDonald's with whatever hotties we'd picked up that night.

It's important to note that while in some ways my teenage years were a nonstop party, I also worked during high school. I'd watched my mother commit to her own career my entire life, so I was inspired to start early on mine. Mahopac is a small town, so I always knew I wanted to get out eventually. Not that my small town wasn't great, but I knew I was destined for something beyond a white picket fence. I grew up reading *Vogue* and *Harper's Bazaar*, and taking trips to the big city. My Happily Ever After was to be filled with culture, travel, and a *career*.

My immediate goal was to work in a high-end store, so my first foray was Stein's Shoes in Mount Kisco, New York. It was super-fancy, and I spent every dollar of my paychecks on swanky footwear. It was here I learned all about amazing shoes, and to judge people for wearing shitty ones. It was also a very competitive sales environment, and I wanted to fit in so badly. The majority of the saleswomen were my mother's age and didn't appreciate a seventeen-year-old coming in and stealing their customers. So instead of helping me and boosting me up, they resented me. Literally, they treated me like I had Ebola; they would look right through me and give me all the shit work. So I did it. I understood I was the low woman on the totem pole and had to pay my dues. I mean, I was making $350 a week, which was a lot of money at the time, and this was where I learned to invest my money wisely à la Carrie Bradshaw—in my closet.

To add insult to injury, many of the men who worked at Stein's were predatory. These old, married men would come on to me. After work we would all go out dancing or to bars, and the men would offer me cocaine, which I never did. Some of these guys had children my age and they wanted to sleep with me. It was, to put it lightly, a really unconventional work environment. The eighties were seriously sick times, when you could sexually harass young girls and no one gave a shit.

Eventually, things got bad enough with the sales competition that the women didn't want me around in Mount Kisco, and I was banished to the other Stein's store, in Pleasantville, New York. Of course the store manager there, Victor, was this hot Latin guy, and he came on to me too. This one I didn't mind as much; he smelled good, loved disco, and had a cool accent. I happen to love dark and sexy inappropriate men. We would fool around, and he also started offering me cocaine. Must have been company policy. I was smart enough to know not to do drugs, especially with a shoe salesman—*duh!* Now, if he had been some hot musician, all bets would've been off.

That year at the company Christmas party I found out that Victor was married and his wife was pregnant. News to me, considering he never wore a wedding ring. That was creepy as fuck. I let him know I never wanted to see him again, and I told one of the other managers that I wanted to go back to Mount Kisco. He was actually a really nice guy, and he threatened Victor's life. I wish Victor had gotten fired, but hey, he had a kid on the way and a coke habit to support—who said I don't have a heart?

Right after the holidays, there was a big end-of-the-season sale and I made $750. My grandparents were so proud of me. Stan, the top-selling salesman, was also so proud of me, and gave me a great big hug. I hugged him back, and he clutched his chest with glee . . . or so I thought. He actually had a massive heart attack and was rushed away via ambulance. I took this as a sign from above to take all my money and run—a come-to-Jesus moment. I had basically almost killed a guy and "stolen" money out of old wenches' mouths, all while being harassed by cocaine addicts. So the next day, driving to work, I kept going right past Stein's and never showed up again. It was like all the dirt was washed off me just by missing the exit off the Saw Mill River Parkway.

It was a Saturday morning, and I went directly to Bloomingdale's in White Plains to apply for a new job, which I got immediately. I came in perky, blonde, and wearing a pale-pink sweatsuit onesie with matching pink pumps. Who wouldn't hire me? The people in Human Resources thought I was so fun and adorable, they assigned me to the fine jewelry department. I loved everything sparkly and expensive, so I knew this was the place for me, no old wenches or cocaine in sight. I immediately called Stubs and told her that she had to come join me at Bloomingdale's. I could not live without her, and roping her into my harebrained ideas was my specialty. Poor Stubs got relegated to the dumpy, middle-aged women's department. She was like, "This is so typical. I'm carrying the crappy clothing and you're the Swatch girl!" It was the best move I ever made; I was out of my town working, making money, and getting the employee discount. I stayed there for about two years, until this great woman, Nicole Bink, came to work in the department. She was about twelve years older than me, very pretty, and lots of fun. We became fast friends. Nicole realized retail wasn't quite for her, but she didn't want to leave me behind. She told me her husband was the general manager at a country club in Rye, New York, and said, "You can work there!"

So Nicole took me to meet her husband, Jack; he was really handsome and about two decades older than I was. He gave me a job serving cocktails on the beach. A lot of the members lived on the beach club grounds, with amazing homes containing Picassos and Renoirs. I knew that *this* was where I belonged! It was all very Waspy but I was a New York City club girl, so I immediately flattened my platinum-blonde punk hair and donned my preppy whites with pride. I really didn't look like a Muffy or, especially, sound like one when I opened my mouth, but *when in Rome*. I did what I had to do to get the job done, and called in my backup, Stubs, and got her a job there too!

One late night at the club, Nicole's husband, Jack, came on to me. Now, I will say it, maybe there was an energy I put out there—but I definitely did not start it. I wasn't flirtatious with him. I didn't try to talk to him. He came over to me. I was like, *You are married to my girlfriend, get away from me*. He said, "Nicole and I aren't happy. She's moving out." I told him that if Nicole actually moved out, that would be a whole other story, but until then, I wasn't playing his game. I had no idea what the fuck was going on. But like I said, he *was* exceptionally good-looking, very nice, and a recovering alcoholic who drank way too much coffee and smoked incessantly. Shockingly, he had white teeth and good breath; I notice these things—good teeth are a social responsibility in my book.

Fast-forward a week, and Nicole does move out. It was over between them. She called me, and the first thing I thought was, *Holy shit, Nicole found out that Jack hit on me*. Only that wasn't it. She said, "Margaret, I just want to tell you before you come to work, I'm moving out. Jack and I are over." As it turned out, she was actually cheating on him and ran away with someone else. Well, that was a relief. Jack was like, *See, I told you*. Very quickly, I graduated from serving cocktails on the beach to having cocktails served to me on the roof deck. Poor Stubs; at least she could have lunch with me on her break while I worked on my tan. I never had to work there again, but the paychecks still kept coming. I was the queen of the country club.

Unfortunately, I couldn't be a kept woman forever. I had to get back to reality and get ready for college. My SAT scores were very good, shockingly, because I barely went to school. Marge Sr. would go to work early in the morning; I would lie and say I was taking the bus, and then sleep late and hitchhike, which was absolutely nuts. Guys in Camaros would pick me up in our small town and deliver me safely to the high school unharmed. It's amazing I never wound up on the back of a milk carton.

I was also notorious for cutting class; I could wallpaper my entire house with the amount of cut slips I got. I was more of a self-taught student. Class felt optional because I could just study the night before and manage to memorize it all. That being said, my homework grades were atrocious. I felt like I should be rewarded for being so naturally smart. This could be considered faulty logic or simply genius; I'll let you decide.

As we were nearing the end of the year, there was a chance I wasn't going to graduate because I was cutting gym so much. It would have been a different story if they'd had acceptable shower facilities and given me time to blow-dry my hair. I am not into swamp ass. So if I was cutting gym, Stubs cut gym too, because I was a very bad influence. I would make her go shopping at Bloomingdale's instead or out to lunch—anything not to sweat. I wasn't too worried about the idea of failing gym because I obviously had something in my back pocket: *If you haven't figured it out yet, I'm not a dope.* My dear friend Laura and I had run into Mr. Mortadella, our gym teacher, when we were out late one night at a club with our fake IDs. He was a little too happy to see us and buy us drinks. He danced with us a bit too close, and then I went in for the kill. I said, "I am never going to gym again, got it, Joe?" Where did I get this chutzpah? He really had no choice but to agree, since he got Laura hammered and I was completely lucid. She puked the whole way home. I thought the least he could do was pass us in gym, right?

It felt like good enough blackmail, but you could never be too sure. So naturally I enacted Plan B to be safe. Fortunately nothing was computerized at the time, and I had friends in high places. Peter Petrinelli was a Dudley Do-Right ass-kissing office-lady lover. Not that that mattered to me. I told him, "As one of my dear friends, you better sneak into the main office and steal our cut slips." I said, "You have to or we're not going to graduate." Stubs was outside crying hysterically, and I was laughing hysterically. I have that reaction when other people get hysterical: I laugh in their face—probably not one of my best qualities. After I stopped laughing, I reassured her that we were absolutely going to graduate. Thankfully, I was right, and if worse came to worst we could dial in the blackmail on Mr. Mortadella.

It was college crunch time, and kids were filling out applications like they were lottery tickets. I knew that fashion was the place for me, and the way to get there was through FIT. So I sent the one application and crossed my Liberace fingers. Stubs was going to the University of Massachusetts, but I knew I wanted to be in New York City. In hindsight it would have been nice if Marge Sr. had guided me or pushed me a little harder. Between my hypochondria and my knowledge of the entire medical encyclopedia, I could have been a great doctor. Thankfully, I got into FIT. My grandparents were thrilled, which was very important to me. Though my mother managed to go back to college as an adult, I was the first generation to attend and graduate.

Unfortunately, in February, before I could graduate high school, my grandfather died. My mother and I were completely devastated. He truly was the rock in our family and had swooped in to save us many times. The perfect daddy to my mother and grandfather to me. My grandmother was equally heartbroken and died a few months later because she could not live without him. With all this death and upset there was only one thing left to do . . . go on a first-class trip to Europe and spend all my grandparents' hard-earned money.

I'm sure they were rolling in their graves, cursing in Hungarian. Marge Sr. invested most of her inheritance in a whirlwind European vacation. We obviously couldn't leave Stubs behind, so off we went on a shopping spree to Paris. We flew first class and traveled for three weeks to France and Hungary to see my mother's family. We also went to Germany to visit my grandfather's sister.

We were Americans in Europe looking for the entire experience—new hair, new clothes, new guys. First stop: Paris. Marge Sr. wanted to take us on a cultural immersion at the Louvre, but I had other plans. So off Marge Sr. went, leaving us the cash to go get Parisian glam. We found the chicest hair salon to perfect my platinum blonde and give Stubs a new European look . . . but something got lost in translation. Although the guidebook stated that this salon had an English-speaking stylist, when we arrived we quickly found out that was not the case. Luckily "Marilyn Monroe" is the universal code for blonde bombshell. Stubs didn't want Marilyn Monroe, but they didn't care what she wanted. While they added the finishing spray to my bouncy blonde blow-dry, screams of *"NO LA MÈCHE! NO LA MÈCHE!!"* echoed through the salon as Stubs sat burning beneath the highlight cap. Her dark Irish hair had turned an unexpected strawberry blonde. She was the talk of the salon, for all the wrong reasons. Everyone was nervously peering around the corner to catch a glimpse. As if this wasn't torture enough, I figured there was no time like the present to take Stubs for her first bikini wax. She was extremely apprehensive, so I took hold of one leg while the waxer took hold of the other. She screamed and squirmed but came out smooth like a newborn baby, and has remained so ever since.

Next stop: Budapest. We were out one night when we stumbled into a group of Marines from the American Embassy. I left the Halászbástya, a famous monument known to the Americans as the Fisherman's Bastion, with the hottest Marine I could find. Stubs slept with some wrestler—whom we also found at the Halászbástya. I remember all their names, but I'll keep some secret. How do I remember so many people's names? Because I don't fucking drink, that's why!

I begrudgingly left my European tour-de-force to make it back to New York for the start of classes. Though I was ready to go to FIT, I didn't feel like I could move to NYC completely. I didn't want to leave Marge Sr. behind, and to be honest, she kind of guilted me. Still, I didn't let that stop me from having fun. I may not have been living in the city yet, but on average I spent twenty to twenty-four hours a day there. That year I met my best gay friend, Raymond. He became a quick constant in my life. I don't really lose people. I just collect them. He would come home with me to Mahopac, sleep in my waterbed, and tickle my arm every night so I could fall asleep. I would do the same for him. We would tell our sex stories and talk about everything going on in our lives and what our futures looked like. Raymond had always wanted to live abroad, and I dreamed of owning my own company. Now he lives in Berlin! *Dreams do come true.* He still flies in and sleeps over at my house; we still tell sex stories and reminisce over our youth. I cry and beg him to move back; he says, "Relax, Marge, nothing's better than having an international best gay in couture."

Raymond and I would tear up Fifth Avenue on a regular basis. Of course, I had a limitless gold American Express card from Marge Sr. that I would charge up with endless trips to Saks Fifth Avenue and dinners all over NYC. My friends couldn't believe it, and I don't know how the hell my mother afforded it. But Marge Sr. would never complain about money, though she should have, because sometimes she couldn't pay our bills. It should have clicked with me, but I was busy at Barneys.

It was required at FIT for juniors to get an internship for college credit. Fortunately, my girlfriend Lisa Sutton's older brother, Larry, was the head of B. Altman, so he was able to get me a job. It was an old-world-luxury Fifth Avenue department store that smelled just like rich old lady. It should come as no surprise that Larry Sutton had a thing for young girls, based on every other man of authority I have worked for. The redeeming thing was I was making the most money out of all my friends and getting a discount. It wasn't your standard internship; on the weekends, I got to work in Larry's office. Lucky me.

Larry was a little man—obviously short guys with facial hair have a thing for me—and he started asking me to dinner. It's always flattering when a powerful man comes on to you, except when it's your married boss who's also your friend's brother. Was I attracted to him? No. Was I interested in sleeping with him? No. But I felt like it was part of the deal. I had to have sex with him to maintain my cushy situation. It was implied and awkward; he had the upper hand: He was my boss. I needed the credits and it took five minutes. It didn't seem like a big price to pay at the time, but over the years these things stay with you. You can't wash them away.

As if sleeping with Larry wasn't insane enough, he had a counterpart named Ronnie Gregory, who was a very handsome Black man, and who was also married. He was like six-foot-three. They both had Porsches and were always in competition with each other. Ronnie also had a thing for me; he would offer to pick me up from school. I took the rides and some free dinners, but I never slept with him. It was very bizarre the way they competed for me. Thankfully, Larry was also screwing my girlfriend Cara, so I told him he should be with her. Eventually, Larry left to be the director of a French fashion house and took Cara with him. Then he started fooling around behind Cara's back with another woman and lost his position there. Shocking. You would think the French would be more liberal. He was actually a nice guy, albeit a serial abuser of power with sex. It's a tough position for a woman to be in. If you say no, you're afraid you could be fired. Thankfully, I've learned how to handle situations like this a lot better with age and therapy. Fortunately, society is beginning to shine light on this intolerable behavior, giving more people the confidence to speak up.

Life Lesson

✦ You will be put in situations that you're uncomfortable with; don't let fear paralyze you. Make the best decision you can in the moment and move on.

Chapter Four

GARMENT-AL GIRL

In my senior year of college I met an Italian rugby player, Luca. What I liked about Luca was that he was sexy and manly; he was actually a Marine for a while. He was also smart, very well read, and older. I had a thing for older men, being mature beyond my years. I was used to being around adults. I didn't have patience for people who were pedantic. I didn't need shallow conversation.

The problem was, I later found out that Luca was totally nuts, controlling, and emotionally abusive. A real fucking asshole.

Being the asshole lover that I am, I decided to get engaged to Luca after a year of dating. Why would I want to do that? Maybe I wanted to break free of my insane life and stop the crazy feeling of being afraid to say no to powerful men. If I was married, that could be an excuse, right? Also, I thought maybe I'd feel less responsible for Marge Sr. I'd be able to start my own life, free and separate from anyone else, and make my own perfect family.

So I took the big diamond ring, which happened to be a stunning trillion stone. Very modern, but not classic. *Not* my style now. But Luca was into nice jewelry, and he wanted to seal the deal before we went home to Italy to see his family; they lived in Pordenone, right outside of Venice. My plan was to take the summer off and not work until that fall.

We were completely passionate about each other . . . passionately getting into screaming matches every chance we had. The worst part about it was that every time we'd have an argument, my mother would take his side, because she was accustomed to being subservient and verbally abused by men. In turn, I was starting to get much more of a backbone. I was sick of being pushed down by men who were trying to take advantage of me, be it in business or sexually, which I did allow for reasons that I needed to really dive into. I was a young girl but with the history of a woman eighty years old.

I thought it was very bizarre that my mother would support Luca over me. I mean, you want your parents to be protective of you. I was like, *Mom, what the fuck are you doing?* It's not like Luca was even so great. He was a loser, especially compared to the rest of his family, who were all established doctors and nice human beings. Unfortunately, Marge Sr.'s past experiences dictated the way she viewed my relationships. But I wasn't going to take it.

Still, Luca and I had a wedding planned for New Year's Eve at Tappan Hill, in Tarrytown, New York. Who cares if I wasn't happy? I had the social event of the year to plan.

We boarded Alitalia and touched down hours later in Venice. I hopped off the plane perky and excited, but it only took Luca *cinque minuti* to make me want to turn around. He walked twenty paces ahead of me, letting me drag my own bags through the airport and across the square while his father looked down from their penthouse terrace. He yelled down at Luca, "Why are you making her drag her own suitcases?" I should have known he wasn't for me right then and there. I mean, look at me, do you think I pack light? Joe would *never*!

There was so much culture to take in and food to inhale that I wasn't going to let Luca's behavior ruin a good trip. Not that his increasingly male-chauvinist, obnoxious, crazy pig behavior wasn't weighing heavily on me. He was insanely jealous of all my previous relationships and would belittle me, calling me *nothing but a receptacle of semen*. He also thought 128 pounds was a little curvy for his five-foot-five fiancée. Coming from someone whose doppelgänger was Eddie Munster, I'm not sure where he got his confidence. After six weeks of *burrata* and berating, I came home and had a little talk with the inner Marge. *I'm not doing this shit. This guy has no drive, and the only upside is his family who lives on the other side of the Atlantic.* I had to lose 180 pounds fast.

I had no qualms with dropping the deadweight; the only issues were (1) losing the wedding deposit, and (2) telling Marge Sr. Of course she didn't take it well. She was like, "He just took you on this beautiful Italian vacation! You adore his family . . ." I was like, "*And?* Big fucking deal. I can't stand him. This is the guy who couldn't even make it to my college graduation on time and then managed to blame it on me." She didn't seem to understand, but she eventually acquiesced to my decision.

Luca, however, did not. There was some serious pushback. At first, he tried begging and groveling, which quickly escalated to yelling and bullying, and culminated in pushing and shoving. I wasn't going to tolerate this insane behavior, so in true Marge fashion I went out to 7 Willow Street (my favorite nightclub) and, to the sound of a live band, picked up my next victim.

Once Luca was out of the picture, I got my first real job, at Toledo Apparel in the Garment Center at 1400 Broadway. They hired me as a shopper, overseeing trends and retail reports. It was the fall of 1989, and the Garment Center was in its heyday. The Garment Center was all about bribes, big sales, high stakes, parties, and drugs. Bad behavior, good times.

Listen, did I want to go into high fashion? Yes. But that's not where the money was. You had to make for the masses in order to eat with the classes. My boss, Vicki Ferrara, groomed me to be a hard worker, harvested my creativity, and boosted me up amongst the insanity. She was the head designer and an amazing mentor; I credit much of my success to her. We would eat dinner together most nights with her husband, Joe (*yes, another Joe*), at their Madison Avenue apartment. Topics of discussion included style, social circles, and suitable suitors. Now we catch up on style and social circles . . . over soup. Our relationship is the reason that I love to work with young women whom I mentor. Women have come so far in the workplace, but there is still so far to go. As of 2020, women hold only 7.4 percent of the Fortune 500 CEO roles. *That's thirty-seven women.* We must cultivate a new culture; mentoring women in the workplace shouldn't be a novelty—it should be the standard.

If you listen to my podcast, *Caviar Dreams, Tuna Fish Budget*, 90 percent of the guests credit their success to a great mentor. We are nothing without the women who support us.

Then there was the man who hired me; let's call him "Dick." He was like the Jewish Dark Prince, typical Garment Center guy, very thin, dark, wore jeans, which—by the way—all went to the dry cleaner to be compulsively folded. How do I know that? Because he lured me back to his apartment after the first few days. He was supposed to show me the ropes, and he showed me a lot more than that. He insisted he needed to make a stop at his apartment near Bloomingdale's after our long day of shopping. He immediately pressed his namesake against me and started kissing me. I panicked, didn't know what to do, and said, "Whoa, slow your roll." He was like, "What's the big deal? We're working together. I'm single, I can make your life very easy." Again, I felt like I had no choice. Now, at this point, you're all probably thinking, *Wow, you were a slut*, but I was thinking, *Why do I feel like I can't say no? What am I afraid of?* I was so headstrong in my convictions, but this was a mind fuck.

Sadly, it takes me back to when I was twelve and all I wanted to do was hang out with my friend Kelly, who was a cute, chubby little ginger baton twirler. Her parents were also divorced and she was on her own quite a bit. Kelly was part of a dance troupe called Honey and the Honey Bees. Honey, the troupe leader, the Abby Lee Miller of her time, would have all the "Little Bees" sleep at her house and get full infiltration into the baton-twirling world. Little did I know the kind of batons that they were twirling. Kelly invited me to sleep over one weekend and I couldn't wait to go. My mother wasn't keen on the idea—maybe she had a premonition—but off I went.

Kelly couldn't wait to introduce me, her little waif friend with budding boobs and short cutoffs. I watched the "Hive" practice their latest routine with Honey's teenage sons. They were handsome in a trailer park way—tall, thin, long hair, skinny mustaches, slightly crooked teeth, and sinewy defined muscles. Much too old to be hanging around prepubescent girls. They ranged in age from seventeen to twenty. They hung on every word I said, flirted with me, picked me up on their shoulders, roughhoused with me, and gave me rug burns. Thinking back, they were probably trying to cop a feel; and boy did they get one. Later that night, one of Honey's sons, Johnny, came into where I was sleeping and woke me with his hard baton on my skinny little leg. He said, "Let me teach you how to make a boy happy." Now, everyone knows I am not easily jarred from sleep, unless it's with coffee and the promise of pastry. I was groggy as he put my little hand down his pants and made me jerk him off. He told me not to tell anyone, that he had a girlfriend. He turned it on me and said that if I told anyone, it would hurt her. I was freaking twelve, what the fuck did I know? I felt as dirty as the mattress on the floor that I was sleeping on.

I questioned whether I'd brought his actions upon myself. Did I give him a sign of some sort? At just twelve years old, I had shame that I was responsible for a man abusing me. I never told my mother, for fear she wouldn't let me see Kelly again and for fear she would think I had somehow provoked him, because that's what goes through your head. You can't believe what's happening, so you think it must be your fault. That's exactly what abusers want.

So years later, with "Dick," the same feelings came back. Had I said something that gave him the wrong impression? It was standard PTSD. I knew what was happening was wrong. I knew he was taking advantage of his power, but I was a grown adult and I could compartmentalize. In a slight defense of "Dick," this was the eighties and there was no Me Too movement yet. His behavior was commonplace—no one spoke up and, unfortunately, it was something women just dealt with.

Meanwhile, I loved my big boss, Damian Schwartz. He would be chauffeured to work every day in his Rolls-Royce Silver Cloud and would hold meetings in his underwear. He didn't like to get his clothes wrinkled, so when he got to the office he would immediately take off his pants and wait for one of the sample makers to come in and press them. He never wore the same underwear twice and would send someone to Macy's weekly to buy him new pairs. OCD was a common running theme in the Garment Center. I became very accustomed to seeing Damian half-dressed and never found it offensive. He also had his own private bathroom, which a very few select people were allowed to use. I happened to be one of them because I was meticulous, and I never shit on the job. If you were one of the chosen ones, you would have to put Efferdent in the toilet to keep the water blue. I thought that was a very good idea. Although one time I forgot to put the Efferdent in, and I was banished from that bathroom for a week.

Damian also had some condition with his eyes and was fearful of putting eyedrops in them, so one of my duties was to do it for him. I would hold his head back and my hand would immediately reek of his cologne, which he would squirt in his face five times a day. He would wiggle around like a five-year-old, but I would get those eyedrops in; he credits me with saving his vision, which is why he was devoted to me. We were very close. I was also one of the only other people who was allowed to drive his Rolls-Royce. It was a totally weird codependent father/daughter relationship.

Often, Damian would scream at me, *You blonde bimbo, come in here!* Though he said it with love and a smile. I never felt taken advantage of. If a boss did that nowadays, it would be completely insulting. "Dick," on the other hand, did take advantage and has acted without boundaries ever since. Even years later, when I ran into him on an airplane, he made sure to bend down to my four-year-old son's level to let him know that his daddy, Jan, was jealous of him. *The delusion . . .*

My other boss, Jimmy Addio, had a penchant for women too. Luckily, I wasn't his type, and thank God, because he looked like Sonny Bono. He was married to a woman named Tammy. They had four children together, but he would only see her on Sundays. Why? Because he actually had another "wife," Cindy, who was a fit model. She was the mother of his other two children. They lived in a big, beautiful home, and he would be with her at all times . . . except Sunday. She was his preferred plus-one to all events, including my wedding to Jan. Jimmy also got Franny, one of the warehouse girls, pregnant. She named her beautiful son Jimmy after his father. I truly don't understand how he managed to attract so many women looking like Sonny.

In retrospect, there were so many things that went down in those days that would be considered inappropriate and illegal now, but then they were considered status quo and part of business. We all knew Thursday nights were reserved for late dinners and Russian hookers. Monday mornings I would get the cash out for bribes or, as we liked to call them, "gifts" for buyers. Wednesday afternoons Jimmy Addio would see "fit models" and check out their measurements in the nude. Should I go on?

I can't decide if those days were easier or harder because no one was fearful of anything and bad behavior was transparent. You always knew what you were going to get. No hidden agenda.

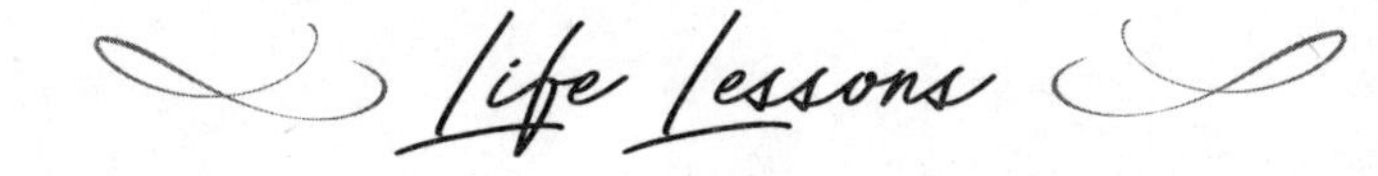

- The only way to break the cycle of abusive behavior is to find the courage to speak up and seek help. It's never too late.
- Find a mentor who sees as much in you as you do in them.

Chapter Five

DADDY ISSUES . . . NOT

What happens when a handsome Jewish lace and embroidery salesman walks into a showroom and spots a pretty shiksa girl twenty years younger? In my case, they fall in love, get married, and raise a family together.

Of course, when I first met Jan, I already had an amazing boyfriend named Harrison James, who was studying to be an attorney. Harrison grew up in Larchmont, New York; his father was an orthopedic surgeon, and he had a house in Martha's Vineyard. He was just perfect, everything you'd want. But I fucked it up. Because who wouldn't prefer a single father of three children from Tenafly, New Jersey?

Jan was salesman extraordinaire at Josephs Brothers Embroidery, his family business. He came into the office to meet with Vicki Ferrara, with his sideswept hair to cover his bald spot, and apparently I was like, *That's the guy for me!* Not really, but Harrison was returning to Tulane Law School after the summer. And you know the old expression—*while the cat's away . . .*

Jan was very flirtatious with me, charming, and funny in his sarcastic way. So I saw the potential (despite the side-sweep). By late August, Jan and I had been doing business together for a while, and he was like, "Why don't we have dinner?" With Harrison's nose in his law books, I agreed, and we decided to meet in the parking lot of the Hilton Hotel in Tarrytown, since I was living in Westchester at this time. I was parked in one spot and he was parked in another. I thought he was a no-show. I was like, *This loser is going to stand me up?* Obviously, I didn't have a cell phone then. I mean, this was 1991! As I was about to write him off, I caught that little bald spot gleaming across the parking lot.

At dinner Jan told me all about "his house" in the Hamptons (his brother's house), and his kids who were at sleepaway camp. In my mind I was thinking, *This guy looks a little young to be having three kids* . . . Later I found out he was two decades my senior. He looked good for forty-four. The date was going well, as far as first dates go . . . until he committed the *ultimate* no-no. Jan said, "Oh, you didn't eat all your dinner. You want to take home a doggie bag?" I was immediately repulsed. Who tells someone on their first date to take home their leftovers?! I'm like, *This guy is cheap. He's not for The Marge.*

But I continued to date him. He was persistent, and the dry humor was starting to grow on me. Things were getting serious, and Jan insisted that I lose the age-appropriate lawyer-to-be. Jan actually drove me to the airport so I could fly to New Orleans to do it in person. Naturally my mother didn't understand why I would leave Harrison for Jan . . . and neither did Harrison. *You're leaving me for a man my father's age??* The guy had a point . . . so I got back on the plane and kept the two boyfriends. When Harrison came home and found out that I was still with "Jan Josephs, King of Embroidery," he drove to my house in a fit of rage to throw rocks at my window and threats at Jan. Jan was panicking, I was simultaneously laughing and crying, and Marge Sr. was trying to let Harrison in the front door. Jan was most concerned that Harrison could read the name of his company on his minivan and would slice his tires. I mean, seriously, you can't make this shit up.

I've thought long and hard about what I saw in Jan. I was young, with a bright future. I did like older men, but not because I never had a father. I think that's too obvious. I've had plenty of boyfriends my own age; I was just more worldly than most of them. My interests were different. My whole life had been one big party with Marge Sr., and now I was taking care of her like a child. I was ready for stability of my own, and Jan filled that role.

When I met Jan, I was at a pivotal point in my life. I was not carefree. I was back living with Marge Sr. in Tarrytown. Her married boyfriend, Joe, had broken up with her and her long-term career had just ended, and the combination of these things sent her into a breakdown. Later she would be diagnosed as bipolar. We tend to see our parents as just that—our parents. You never think anything can be *really* wrong because they're the ones who take care of you. In any case, I saw that Marge Sr. needed me, even if she couldn't verbalize it. So I was paying most of the rent and giving her money to get her back on her feet. I felt a responsibility to save her. I'm sure she feels badly about it now, but she wasn't able to acknowledge it back then.

My help was just expected. This is Marge Sr.'s story to tell, and now looking back, I can see that she did the best she could and held it together amazingly well, all things considered. Though she gives me PTSD some days, she has made up for it tenfold by being the best grandmother to my son and the best friend a daughter could have.

When Jan came into my life, I was happy, but something *was* missing. I was thriving in my career, but at the same time I was yearning for a family of my own. I knew my career was going places, and I loved that it allowed me financial freedom. From a young age I was determined not to have to rely on anyone else for my well-being. I knew my happiness lay within. Jan seemed like a great partner to complete the familial package I desired.

It was very important for me to be with someone who was an amazing father, especially since my father wasn't around when I was growing up. It was equally essential for my partner in life to be a hard worker, and Jan really fit the bill. He had full custody of his three children, which is very rare. His crazy ex-wife had given up custody of her own kids to move to Florida and start a new life as a gossip columnist. Later I found out that she delegated the writing of the articles to a dear friend of mine but took all the credit anyway. Forge all the articles you want, but I'm going to say it right now: The one area where I *am* judgmental is when it comes to kids. Abandoning your young children for your own selfish gain is something I could never understand. For all my mother's shortcomings, she never left my side or made me feel unloved. The good news is Jan's ex-wife leaving was the best thing for all of us. Any animal can give birth, but it takes a real woman to be a mother, and I was ready.

At this point, Marge Sr. was doing much better, and I was able to move into a beautiful two-bedroom on the Upper East Side on 84th and Lex. I was fully moved in but still living out of a suitcase, since I was spending most nights at Jan's house. He would come pick me up with my stepdaughter, whom I consider my daughter, and then drive me back to New Jersey to sleep at their house. My roommate, Sara, said I was the best ex-wife she ever had. I paid the rent fully and was at my boyfriend's house every night.

He lived in a modern home in Tenafly, New Jersey, that was straight out of the *Knots Landing* cul-de-sac. Google it. Something clicked in the back of my brain when he said Tenafly. I remember as a little girl going over to my friend Kelly's grandmother's house to play, and she said to me, "Kelly's not here today. She's in Tenafly. Do you know where Tenafly is?" I was about ten years old, so I said no. She then told me, "It's a very wealthy area in northern New Jersey. A lot of nice rich people live there." So when Jan said Tenafly, it was very weird, like déjà vu. I'd only heard of that town once before, and I was like, *This is my destiny!* Who doesn't like rich people who are nice?

Everybody says it's very hard with stepchildren—that they're not going to like you right away—but it only took them about two weeks to warm up to me. They were naturally starved for maternal attention; they needed me and I needed them.

I quickly traded the taxis for a minivan. Jan's daughter, Tori, was eight years old, and the two boys, Dean and Bret, were fourteen and sixteen. Though I looked more like the hot nanny, I was settling into my new role of stepmom-to-be. The rest of Jan's family quickly warmed up to me as well. I wasn't the Jewish girl they had hoped for, but it hadn't worked out so well the first time, so why not switch it up? Eight months after practically living there, I decided to make the full move. I took whatever little was left in my NYC apartment and relocated to Tenafly to live with my new family.

I was still working in the Garment Center, making good money, but—even though we weren't married yet—I devoted my whole life to Jan's children, running kids to Bar Mitzvahs and styling little girls' hair. Don't get me wrong, I had full-time live-in help as well.

Tenafly wasn't the easiest town to move into. It's still not. At first, the other mothers were like, *Oh my God, who is this young blonde vixen that Jan is dating?* I mean, I *was* a young blonde vixen. But, pretty quickly, they accepted me. Despite my affection for the male species, I've always gotten along with women very well.

The funny thing is that my mother and Jan are actually only one year apart in age. Marge Sr.'s date of birth is September 7, 1946, and Jan's is September 5, 1947. The truth is, he could easily have been dating Marge Sr. Fortunately, Jan was extremely immature, I was extremely mature, and Marge Sr. wasn't in the market for a stable family man. They had a combative relationship from the start. Marge Sr. definitely does not have a filter and is not the best with boundaries. Jan does not have a filter and is not the best with boundaries either, hence the problem.

In my mother's defense, I believe that she wanted me to have a fairy-tale life. I don't think that fairy tale included me mothering three children at the young age of twenty-four. In Jan's defense, he was used to a traditional parental relationship, and he wasn't bargaining on a package deal with me and Marge Sr. I often felt like the referee between the two of them. They both could have used some time in the penalty box.

I was comfortably settling into my new life of suburbia. I traded nightclubs for PTA clubs. I'd fucked enough guys at this point that I didn't need to sleep with anybody else. And I knew I wanted to get pregnant in the not-so-distant future. So, one day I said to Jan, "I hope you know we have to have a kid one day." He replied, too quickly, I might add, "I'm not having any more kids. I have three already and that's enough." I said, "Oh, you're not having any more kids? Then you're not having me. I'm leaving right this second." All I had to do was take some clothes out of the closet and put them in my car, and Jan was holding on to my bumper for dear life. It took all of ten minutes to change his mind: "Okay, fine, I'll have another baby." I was on a roll, so I doubled down with "You know we'll eventually have to get married too." He got the message loud and clear.

Not long after came the very romantic proposal. He came home from work one day, pulled a ring out of his pocket, and said, "Here you go." He followed directions; it was the emerald-cut stone I wanted . . . It could have been a little bigger, considering I was the second wife, but it was gorgeous nonetheless.

Next he brought home a white Lexus for me to drive, and they kept coming every three years. I had no input on the car I drove, not even the color. Jan felt that a Lexus was the appropriate car for his wife-to-be to drive, so that's what I drove. Jan never really expected me to pay for anything . . . except for my clothes, beauty treatments, home décor, gifts for everyone, and anything he found superfluous.

Basically, I paid for a ton of shit. We never had a conversation about finances; rather, I was told how it was going to be and put up with it. We had plenty of money, and I didn't want to rock the boat.

My engagement ring was getting lonely on my finger, so I thought it was about time to start wedding plans. Jan and I had vastly different visions for the occasion. Of course, I wanted a huge celebration; Jan would have been happy to get married in our kitchen over a bowl of pasta. I wanted Jan to fulfill my childhood dream wedding, but if he couldn't do it, I had no choice but to do it myself. He'd done it all before and he hadn't even enjoyed it the first time. So instead, Vicki Ferrara filled in as the groom to help me decide on every detail—except for the food. Jan loves a cocktail wiener more than anyone.

Remember when I said that the superfluous purchases were to be taken care of from my end? Yeah, Jan considered the wedding a superfluous purchase. Jan actually let me foot the bill for the *entire* wedding. This wasn't easy to pull off, but thank God it was the early nineties and the Garment Center was booming, so I was raking it in. I should have seen the red flag, but how could I? I had rose-colored glasses on. I was in love and it was full speed ahead. God knows I love a fabulous party.

Vicki and I landed on November 19, 1994, at the Empire Hotel in NYC. The music makes the party, so I obviously booked a ten-piece band for my one hundred wedding guests. One musician per ten guests. That's my rule. The flowers were abundant, in hues of pale pinky peach, white, and gold. The cake? Oh, you know, the obvious: carrot covered in fondant. The last and arguably most important factor: my dress. Traditionally the groom isn't supposed to see you in the gown, but my stand-in groom, Vicki, came to Kleinfeld's with me anyway. I'm not really a traditional girl, so I obviously wasn't going to wear white. Instead I opted for a nude satin under gold lace with tiny little rhinestones and a gorgeous shimmery gold tulle ball gown skirt, designed by Rose Taft. Vicki said, "You look like Eva Perón with your platinum-blonde hair and red lipstick." Well, I could definitely rule a small country, if not Argentina . . .

It was an intimate affair, just our family, close friends, and everybody we worked with in the Garment Center. Marge Sr. obviously wore a white Rose Taft gown . . . as the mother of the bride. My two stepsons—though I call them my sons—walked me down the aisle and gave me away. My daughter and niece were little flower girls. Judy, my best friend, was the maid of honor. Her brother also attended. Remember Chris? The guy I first had sex with? You might be surprised he was invited, but actually he wasn't the only (s)ex in attendance. There were about four others, but I won't name them. It's in the Top 10 best days of my life—I still watch the wedding video and tear up . . . I don't think I'll ever look so good again.

We danced till dawn and counted the checks in the morning. Everyone was extremely generous, especially my in-laws. It was quite a substantial sum, and since I'd already paid for the entire wedding, Jan was like, *Keep the money and buy whatever you want for the house.* Gee, thanks.

We left two days later for our weeklong honeymoon in Anguilla. Cap Juluca and Malliouhana were the only two resorts worth the trip. We stayed in a beautiful villa at Cap Juluca, with Janet Jackson next door. I insisted to Jan that we must go to Anguilla, because the restaurant we loved in the Hamptons, Cyril's, had a location there. I was all about going to the most exotic, remote places, which Anguilla was back in November 1994. We were there for Thanksgiving and decided to eat at Malliouhana. Jan was disappointed they served turkey; he was like, *We're in the islands, we should only be eating fish.* Happy Thanksgiving, Debbie Downer.

We had sex every day. The accommodations were beyond luxurious. The food was delicious. We had massages. Naps on the beach. A perfect honeymoon, except Jan felt it was *too* relaxing. His famous line was *It's great if you're recovering from heart surgery.* Translation: It was equivalent to a hospital stay. Jan was and still is underwhelmed by everything. If he'd won the lottery, he would have said, *That's great, sweetie, but we have to give half to taxes.*

We returned to suburbia sun-kissed.

- You can love someone so much you hate them; it's a very fine line.
- At the end of the day, a marriage is a contract, and a contract means business.
- Don't mistake naïveté for blind faith. Protect yourself; no one else is going to.

Chapter Six

JUST ADD WATER

Once we'd returned from our honeymoon and our regular life had resumed, I was so happy to be home with the kids and Jan. Any shortcomings I may have detected in our relationship became a nonissue.

Honestly, I had known I was going to marry Jan a few months into dating him. He felt like home, and it was clear to me that being with him was exactly what I needed. To this day, I've never regretted that decision. I truly believe we were meant to be together. Even though our marriage ended up being tumultuous, I learned a lot of lessons during that time.

One of those lessons was to be more aware of financial arrangements. Here I was, living in Tenafly, in this amazing house that I'd decorated, taking care of my husband and his three kids, and Jan never even put my name on the deed. He owned the house outright. Not only that, but Jan made me keep a separate bank account. He thought it was the most prudent way to do things because he'd had so many money problems with his ex-wife, Eviline, whom we paid a large chunk of change to. Jan was always worried about money, even though he didn't need to be. I mean, we had two successful careers and full-time help. Regardless, he was completely neurotic about it. And I didn't know any better. I'd never been married before, nor did I have a parent who could guide me. I asked a few times for us to buy a new home together so I could own something. Jan would always say, *Sweetie, don't worry, I have life insurance, you'll be fine*. So I gladly spent my own salary on things for the house, clothing for myself, and stuff for the children. I created a beautiful home for all of us. In the meantime, Jan would only buy me gifts on holidays; he wasn't very thoughtful. I was the thoughtful one. I always made sure to do the right thing by everybody. Fortunately, my in-laws were extremely generous. They paid for many things, including my children's sleepaway camp.

We led a very charmed existence, but it was not this billionaire jet-set lifestyle where I was jaunting to the islands on a whim, driving a Mercedes convertible, and playing tennis at the country club. I still worked, which was very important. In hindsight it was good that I made my own money, because Jan wasn't exactly throwing cash in my direction.

At first, everybody talked about us. People would whisper, *Who is this twenty-years-younger, blonde, buxom hussy Jan is parading around with?* When we went on vacation, people would ask Jan if he was having an affair with his secretary! He was like, "That's my wife." It was very funny. I did look younger than him, but I was madly in love, and I think everybody in town knew that. They also saw the way I was devoted to the kids, so ultimately I was very well received by the other mothers and we had some great times. They knew I had no agenda. Believe me, if I was digging for gold, I would not have married Jan Josephs. No one was giving up their personal life and putting things on hold to join a family and take care of three kids. I would never say I gave up my hopes and dreams, but things certainly changed drastically for me.

I no longer hung out with my old friends, who were my age. My friends were now the people I worked with and the parents of the other kids at school. My Saturdays were spent watching my daughter play Biddy Basketball.

I was an instant mom, and my whole life became about the kids. I loved them like they were my own from day one. I will say that when I came into that house there was tumult. The boys would fight. Jan would be screaming. You can ask him or anybody in that town, and they'll tell you that I brought a sense of peace and calm to that family. I would not tolerate Jan ever hitting the kids, which he sometimes had when things had gotten out of hand, but never again once I moved in.

Even though I was just a young girl myself, I was the kids' full-time mother. Their "birth mother"—which is what I prefer to call Eviline—only showed up on Mother's Day, and then behaved like she was Mom of the Year. I'm no doctor, but I've seen prescription drug abuse, and she fit the criteria, in my opinion. I mean, can you imagine abandoning your own children and moving far away when you have the means to stay close by and watch them grow up? Because that's what she did. I find that very selfish. If she did it to get herself healthy, I would have been empathetic. Those kids were in need of maternal attention, and I was the one who was there. I needed someone to give all of my love to, and in turn, they desperately needed to be loved, so it was the ideal combination. Finally, after so many years, I had a family.

Sundays were my favorite. Jan's parents would come over, and my brother-in-law and sister-in-law would drive over the bridge from the city. I would cook a huge dinner. My father-in-law loved my meatballs. It was a very homey, happy feeling. There was always a lot of hoopla. It was absolute craziness, but in a good way.

Then the next morning I would get up, Jan would drive me to the bus stop near his embroidery factory in West New York, New Jersey, and I would take the bus into Manhattan. We would sneak out during the day and have coffee together in the Garment Center, and then he would wait for me on 38th Street, at the side of my building, and we would carpool home together just in time for family dinner with the kids. It really was perfect.

It was a fun time in our lives. In the summertime we'd ship the kids off to sleepaway camp and spend our weekends in the Hamptons going out to dinner every night. But I would be so excited on visiting day to go up and see the kids at camp. I would miss them. I would write letters to them every week. It was everything I'd ever wanted.

Marge Sr. was also around during this time. She ate dinners with us on Sundays. She loved the kids and was extremely attentive to them. She would dote on them, hang out with them, and buy them gifts. My mother felt they were her grandchildren, even if not genetically. It was an interesting dynamic for me to observe because she'd never been that way as a mother.

Of course Jan was constantly sarcastic to her. This is a very shallow thing to say, but I believe Jan didn't like fat people, and my mother was fat during this period. It was a combination of depression and binge eating. He would say, *Margaret, she's got to lose weight.* He literally couldn't take it. It made me feel badly that he would say that, but he was right, it wasn't healthy. It was part of a long-standing destructive eating pattern of hers, and it took a little while for her to get her health back.

Thankfully, aside from Jan, everyone else was so great to her, including Jan's parents and my brother-in-law and sister-in-law. Still, there was always an undercurrent of distrust between me and Marge Sr. because she wouldn't stop drinking. I would tell her to stop and then everyone would come down on me for it.

No one really understood the history I had with my mother or all the problems her alcohol abuse had caused when I was growing up. Often, I found myself irritated that the rest of the family would insert themselves into the situation. I would say to Marge Sr., *One drink only, slow your roll.* Sometimes I think she'd drink more just to spite me. I never knew whether she was upset about something in the moment or if there was a larger, deeper psychological issue at hand. But I was definitely like, *What the fuck is going on here? And why is everyone pushing me to back off when clearly she has a problem?* My family told me I was a bitch, mean to my mother, basically a buzzkill.

Then Marge Sr. would turn it on me too, like, *Oh, she's the party pooper*. She didn't like me trying to limit her to one glass, and she didn't care that her lack of discipline made me uncomfortable and anxious, so that was not the best scenario. Yet, generally speaking, we were all happy to be together and we always spent the holidays as a family.

I was raised Catholic, but I was an honorary Jewish girl. I did the Jewish holidays better than anyone. I would whip up a huge Rosh Hashanah meal and make a mean brisket for Passover. Yom Kippur "break the fast" was exclusively at my house. For many years we hosted everything; my in-laws were over constantly. I believe they were so happy Jan finally had a wife who loved the family and brought everyone together, as opposed to Eviline, who didn't care much for them. My in-laws now had two amazing daughters-in-law, each very different. My sister-in-law was beautiful in a granola way and a genius, twenty years older than me. Not a big spender, preferred drinking over eating, basically the opposite of me. We got along fabulously. She favored my mother-in-law and I favored my father-in-law. Maybe because he had a penchant for the glamorous, loved my cooking, and saw my magic.

With that said, there was one thing that was nagging at me. I wanted to get pregnant. I knew once that happened, my mother would move back to New Jersey from Westchester, where she was living, and for many reasons I thought that was a good idea. I was on the pill for a long time, and finally, a year after Jan and I were married, I said, *Okay, we're married a year. We've been together since I was twenty-four. I'm now twenty-eight. I want to have a baby.* Of course Jan was just like, *Okay, that's fine*. As per usual, everything was underwhelming to him. I didn't care, though. I knew he'd come around eventually, so I went off the pill and that was it.

Within about two or three months, I was knocked up. I was *thrilled*!!! When I told Jan, I thought he was going to be so elated. I thought he was going to lift me up in the air and kiss me. I even showed him the positive pregnancy test to elicit a reaction. But his only response was "That's great, Margaret."

That's great, Margaret?! What the fuck?! I said, "Jan, that's all you have to say?" He was like, "Yeah. What's the shock? I have three other kids."

Again, that probably should have been another red flag. But I was too blinded by excitement to see it. Yet.

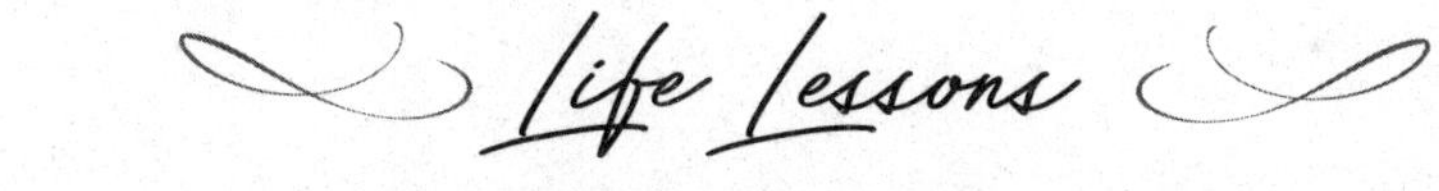

- Motherhood is not defined by the act of labor.
- Sometimes you don't know what you were missing all along until you've found it.

Chapter Seven

ICING ON THE CAKE

I was the most neurotic pregnant woman ever. You would think no one else had ever given birth before me. I guess it was my years of reading the medical encyclopedia. Every second I thought the baby was falling out. I was spotting. I was nervous, and Jan was not one to really coddle my feelings. He was like, *I'm not a doctor, what are you telling me for? Call them.* So I managed to arrange weekly sonograms to calm my nerves. But that didn't stop me from eating. I was totally packing on the pounds—that's the way I made myself feel better, which was fine, because I was a buxom girl. When I got married, I weighed only 127 pounds, and back then, I thought I was fat. I would give my right arm to be 127 pounds again.

When it came time to go for our official sonogram, to find out the sex of the baby, I really wanted a little girl. I only knew about little girls. Jan and I were raising our other kids—a fabulous daughter and two sons—so I thought it would be perfect to have another girl to round out the family. Everyone was like, *Margaret, you look like shit. It must be a daughter stealing your beauty.* How could I not have a little girl? I was going to name her Scarlet or Ruby.

So imagine my surprise when the sonographer said to Jan and me, "Well, do you want to know what you're having?" and I said yes, and she said, "A son." I was like, *What?! Oh my God. I don't know anything about boys.* Jan was like, "What? Look again." I could see the disappointment on his face. He was completely in shock.

I changed my tune pretty quickly. I was like, *Boys love their mothers!* I had the perfect name picked out. *We'll call him Cooper.* I was just so thrilled. But, as soon as we left, I realized that Jan was legitimately freaking out. He was saying things like, *I'm not ready for this. I'm not young. I'm not ready to go to Little League games again. How are we going to do this?* I mean, at this point, I was twenty-eight and Jan was forty-eight. That's a big difference in the way of being a new parent.

It was emotionally draining being pregnant and not feeling Jan's enthusiasm. This was my first natural-born child and would be my last. I envisioned a loving time when we could bond together over Lamaze. But instead I went with my girlfriend Judy, who was also pregnant. Everything that was new to me was old to Jan.

Immediately, it became obvious that he did not want a boy because he expected it would be all his responsibility. He thought he would have to do everything, and he'd already been there and done that with his other sons. I think Jan was having PTSD from his first marriage. He felt like if he had another daughter I would swoop in and take charge. Clearly, he didn't realize that this marriage was different than his last. I did everything for the kids anyway, so I was like, *All right, let's order the crib.*

By the time I had the baby, I was 180 pounds of solid beef. I thought I was giving birth to a real bruiser. I was a natural. I squeaked that kid out with fifteen minutes of pushing. It was so easy. I was like, *What's everyone bitching about? How hard is it to have a baby?* I don't know why, I must have the Lincoln Tunnel between my legs; he just popped right out.

The unfortunate thing for me (and my extra weight) was that Cooper was not that big. He was only six pounds, fifteen ounces, and very tall. I was like, *Why is this kid so little and why am I so fat?* I weighed more than my husband. Can you believe that the day I gave birth, Jan said to me, "Sweetie, you're a house." I remember the nurse commenting that I looked like that famous actress Brett Butler, which I did not take as a compliment. Apparently, neither did Jan. He said, "No, my wife's actually really beautiful. She just happens to look like shit today." I was like, *Thanks, Jan. You're always so complimentary.*

Five minutes after Cooper had arrived, my three other kids joined me and Jan at my bedside, blood still on the floor. Everything we did was a group activity. I wouldn't have it any other way.

When it was time to come home, I didn't want to leave the hospital because everybody was at my house waiting for me—the kids, my in-laws, my mother, and of course the new additions: our baby nurse and au pair, because I had to have a full staff. Jan was adamant about that. There was no way we were doing it on our own. I mean, I didn't know from baby nurses. I didn't grow up that way. Our baby nurse, Grandma Mary, was an elderly little Black woman who wore tons of wigs. She changed my life, and I am forever indebted to her. She taught me everything there was to know about babies. Our au pair, Shauna, from England, was also on hand. There were all these people prepared to help me, but I didn't want anybody to hold my baby. I wanted to stay in the hospital and keep my son all to myself.

I cried the whole way home—the three minutes that we lived from the hospital. Jan was like, *Stop it. What's wrong with you? Everybody's so excited to see you, what the fuck?* He was mad at me. I was like, *Dude, I just had a kid two days ago*. Not to mention that I had given birth with a full face of makeup and expertly applied lipstick. I looked like a fucking rock star. I had held my own freaking legs. Give me a break.

But I sucked it up—there was no other choice. And once we got home, our life just took over. The little prince had arrived. He was the glue that held everybody together. The whole family was immediately obsessed with Cooper. And, luckily for Jan, everything went very smoothly. Cooper quickly became the light of his life; he still is.

Yet, despite all the available help, I didn't want most of it. Baby nurses are supposed to get up with the child in the middle of the night so the mother can rest, but I wasn't having that. If Grandma Mary got up with Cooper, I got up too. We hung out together while I nursed him. I made heavy cream for that kid. I would literally wake up in a puddle of milk. He packed on the pounds in the same way I had when I was pregnant with him.

All I wanted to do was bask in the pure joy I was feeling. Only not everyone was on board with that, namely Jan. Within three weeks of having Cooper, I was expected to be right back on our regular schedule. It was the summer and the Hamptons were calling. I wanted to be able to wear a bikini so badly, but I was still fat as fuck. Did anyone give a shit how I felt, though? No. We went anyway. I put a little bandanna on Cooper's bald head and that was that. I remember feeling gross and unlike my usual self. Conversely, Jan was in perfect shape. He was running all the time. We come from a very shallow family; you're allowed to have a fat ass, but don't ever have a stomach. I had a stomach, and Jan didn't make an exception for Mum Tums. Jan was also a professional tanner. He was a human sundial and would sit on the beach and soak in the rays. It was like no one clued him in to the fact that you can't sunbathe with a newborn. So there I was, sitting under an umbrella in the shade with our baby, like I should have been, and Jan completely ignored me. Honestly, I think he was like, *My wife is a pork chop, she doesn't look as beautiful as she usually does, and I don't want people to think I'm associated with her.*

I would say, "Come over here, come sit by me, help me with the baby." But it became very clear, very quickly, that Jan wasn't going to do that. He felt like I had help, so he didn't have to do any of the heavy lifting. He just wanted to do the fun things like hold him when everyone was doting over how cute he was.

At this point, I really started thinking to myself, *I can't be with this man. I cannot see growing old with him; something is off. This can't be forever. I need someone who's going to nurture me, someone who's going to worship me.* The way that I worshipped Jan and my children. It was a very sad, pivotal moment. I couldn't help but wonder, *How did we get here?*

I will say that I was blessed because my daughter was like a little mother. She was obsessed with Cooper and glued to my leg at all times. It was like she had given birth too. She was so cute wheeling him around in the carriage. I had such a great support system in her, which I'm thankful for to this day.

The three months of maternity leave went by quickly, and I still wasn't ready to leave Cooper. Even though I knew he was going to be in good hands, I dreaded the idea of being away from him all day. But Jan was used to me making a decent amount of money, and he was like, *You're going back to work. That's the deal.* Everything was about this deal he felt we'd made. And the deal was never allowed to shift. He was like, *You said this, you said that.* I couldn't ever change my fucking mind or have any other emotions. He didn't understand that I was a new mother. Plus, it wasn't like my income even paid our main bills. The money I made was *supposedly* for myself. The thing was—and this is what's so interesting—he did not want to feel like he had to support me. His focus was on everything else that needed to be paid for—the nanny, the kids' camp, college—and he believed that anything I wanted was up to me. It was totally ridiculous, because clearly, we weren't starving without my salary. It was a startling realization: I was responsible for myself even though we were married.

So I reluctantly held up my part of the "deal" and headed back to the Garment Center. The first day, I cried like the baby I was leaving behind. At this point I was nearly down to my pre-pregnancy weight. As Marge Sr. would say, *It's better to look good than to feel good.* Vicki was thrilled to have me back. I knew she had worked out a four-day in-office deal, and I was hoping I could manage to get the same gig. That way I could have one day a week at home with Cooper. I asked my boss if I could do the same, but he said, *No, that's not the deal. Just Vicki has that situation.* Needless to say, I wasn't pleased with that answer. My emotions and hormones were out of balance since giving birth. It wasn't postpartum but more of a separation anxiety. I knew Shauna loved Cooper and took good care of him . . . but she just wasn't me.

Luckily, a few months after being back at work, I got sick. That may sound funny, but it was a blessing in disguise. I was constantly dizzy and rapidly losing weight. At first, the doctors thought I had a very strange tumor called a carcinoid tumor. Truly, it was like a gift from God, because then I had to take a sabbatical from work. I was like, *Yay, I might have some bizarre illness, but I get to be with my baby!* And thankfully, it did not turn out to be life-threatening. There was some crazy issue where I'd eaten too many bananas before my blood test, which had thrown off the results. It was a trick I hadn't even realized I was performing. Still, I had to go on medication for my stomach and thyroid, and I was always under the weather. I think my bosses were a little pissed; they definitely weren't very sympathetic. But I packed my bags and exited the premises . . . *Doctor's orders.*

Once my two-month sabbatical was up, I went back to work,

but things had changed. My bosses had opened a new company while I was away, and they said that they could offer me a position there, but I could no longer continue at the current company. The catch was that the budget for the new company meant a slight pay cut of $100 a week for me. I said, *I've been an employee of yours for eight years and I've proven myself. Now you want me to prove myself again for less money? No fucking way.*

Not surprisingly, Jan wanted me to bow down and take that $100-a-week pay cut. I was like, *No, I'm going to take a well-deserved break, collect my unemployment, and spend time with my baby.* Jan wholeheartedly disagreed; he wanted me to be working. *That was the deal, remember?* He couldn't believe the amount of money I was willing to walk away from out of principle. I was tired of the sexual harassment, Russian hooker nights, and wiping my boss's kid's ass.

Unfortunately, the dynamic between me and Jan really shifted once I stopped working. The loss of my income caused Jan to harbor feelings of resentment toward me. We started fighting more and more often. Jan would have a hemorrhage at me over the smallest things. If I misplaced the car keys, it was as if I had killed his parents. Cooper's first birthday party was a disaster. The audacity of me to drive all of four miles to NYC to get a birthday cake. In Jan's opinion: *What psycho case would pay a toll for that?* That was a twenty-minute beratement, which sent me and the au pair into a crying fest, all before the guests arrived. Once everyone was there, we were all smiles, like nothing ever happened. Jan had two pieces of cake—I guess the toll *was* worth it.

It had become obvious to me that Jan was not supportive of a lot of my choices. He never had a sense of how deeply I was feeling about something. In fact, he was very dismissive of the way I felt many times. Though his IQ might have been high, his EQ was very low. Our arguments were explosive; plates flying, doors slamming, screaming, and crying were a weekly occurrence. Many times, I would call on my in-laws to intervene. My father-in-law would come flying over and mediate, saying, *Jan, when she's right, she's right, just stop*. I don't want to make it out like I was innocent, though—it takes two to battle, and I'm not known to be a shrinking violet.

It was a challenging period in our marriage, and to make matters worse, our middle son, Dean, was leaving for college. I was devastated. I cried and held on to him when he left that September, like he was going to war. I felt like a piece of my heart was missing. Cooper was only a few months old, so I couldn't take Dean to his school in Wisconsin, and I was so distraught about that. What was really horrible was that Jan didn't take him either. I thought that was very bizarre. He let Dean go to college for the first time, to move in, with his best friend and his family. Granted, Dean was always extremely independent, but I still felt that Jan should have gone with him. We flew out to visit him as soon as I could and made sure to visit often.

There were so many occasions when I had to teach Jan to do the right thing. Some things just weren't innate to him. I think as we raised Cooper together it let Jan become an even better father to our older kids.

Even with all our issues, we were a great team when it came to parenting. You'd think that their birth mother would appreciate knowing that her children's home life was filled with love, but instead I felt like she resented me for it and treated me like absolute dirt. She actually called the kids and said, "Just wait until Margaret has the baby—she'll never love you or want to be with you again." That was obviously an outright lie. Having Cooper brought the family even closer together, and my love for my children knows no bounds. I'm only as happy as my unhappiest child, and even though today I am estranged from two of them, knowing that they are happy in their lives gives me solace. After all that, Eviline had the audacity to send me a baby gift. I should have broken it over her head. But I took the high road, as I always did. I graciously thanked her for it; I mean, who could turn down a blue box from Tiffany's? In hindsight I should have also thanked her for giving me the gift of motherhood three times over without the extra stretch marks.

After a year of being home with Cooper, I had the itch to be creative and start working again. Though motherhood is extremely fulfilling, my identity is multifaceted. I yearned for an outlet, and let's face it . . . my unemployment had run out. My sister-in-law, Marie, was a producer for commercials. She would sometimes hire me to do freelance styling or makeup on set. I was never formally trained in this, but I'm a quick learner. It was a great way to dip my toe back into the working world. It reignited my drive and got me thinking about starting my own business one day.

Life Lesson

- Motherhood changes your priorities and gives you a new perspective. Be confident in your judgment that you know what is best for you and your child.

Chapter Eight

BIRTH ON THE KITCHEN TABLE

Before I knew it, Cooper was already two and ready for preschool. We decided on Temple Sinai. I wanted Cooper to be raised in the Jewish faith like all his siblings were, even though I am Catholic myself. It was a great program, and even more important, it was only around the corner. So the odds of me getting him there on time were in my favor. Cooper and I were both very late sleepers, so by the time we rolled out of bed it would be a mad rush. I'd quickly make a coffee to get myself going, and Cooper would take some sips too; after all, he's European. On one particularly late morning I accidentally packed bacon in his lunch box, which is definitely *not* kosher at temple. Thankfully they knew he was a picky eater, so they let it slide.

With Cooper in school, I thought it would be a good time to take action on starting my own business. Working for someone else was just not in the cards for me anymore. I reached out to my good friend Beth, who was a previous boyfriend's sister. I kept Beth after the breakup. Like I've said, I don't lose people; I collect them. Beth was an extremely talented artist who'd graduated from Carnegie Mellon. Cooper had the house littered with toys, and I had a bright idea. I wanted to create a stylish storage solution that was utilitarian and fashionable at the same time. Beth and I went to Home Depot and filled the Lexus to the brim with metal buckets. Beth was big into decoupage, so we decided to embellish the buckets with vintage wallpapers. They looked very shabby chic; we thought we were on to something because there was nothing like them available at the time. All the storage solutions were unattractive, and we set out to fix that. We decided to name the company Macbeth Collection—a combination of Margaret and Beth. I often say we gave birth to the Macbeth Collection at my kitchen table.

I had the bigger personality of the two of us, so I said to Beth, "Let me see if I can convince a store in town to carry our buckets." Beth was all for it, so I paid a visit to the hottest kids' boutique in town, Cradle & All, and I gave my best sales pitch, which is hard to resist. They agreed to take eight pieces on consignment. We were sold out in one day. By dinnertime I had a call from the owner, demanding a restock. As we got into more and more stores, I realized the potential we had to corner the market on kids' accessories.

Beth and I were each making a few hundred dollars a week as we expanded into picture frames and other accessories. It was fun and very of the time. Everyone was like, *Oh, how cute, Margaret has a little business of her own*. Perhaps they didn't realize that The Marge was not to be underestimated.

On a whim I put our name on the waitlist for the New York International Gift Show. Careful what you wish for, because all of a sudden we received a letter in the mail saying that Macbeth had been accepted into the show. At this point I started to see Macbeth Collection as more of a full-time career than a side gig. We were momentarily thrilled, until we realized how much work we had to get done. We knew the show was going to be filled with large, established companies, and we wanted to be able to stand out and not look like we belonged at the arts and crafts table. We were going to need to invest all our profits and then some, to even be able to attend.

For that, I had to go to Jan Josephs. As you can imagine, he wasn't thrilled with the idea of funding what he considered to be a hobby. He told me to approach my sister-in-law, Marie. She very generously lent me $8,000, which may not sound like much now, but back then I didn't have access to a dime. I mean, how pathetic. Any personal expenses from that moment on were under the scrutiny of Marie and Jan's brother. In their opinion you shouldn't even get a manicure until you pay back the money in full. They didn't understand that looking polished goes hand in hand with business; everything is about the packaging.

Beth and I showed up at the New York International Gift Show like a band of gypsies with our vintage-curtain backdrops, rolling carts of buckets, and hand-painted tables to decorate our booth with. We thought we were so cool. These were the days in New York City when you could bribe the guys at the front to help you as long as you were cute. All I had to do was flash my cleavage and grease their palms with a hundred bucks, and I could park anywhere. I was all about working smarter, not harder.

The show was at the Piers on the West Side Highway in Manhattan. We drove there with everything but the kitchen sink, or so we thought. When we arrived to see everyone setting up their lights, it dawned on us that we hadn't even ordered electricity. No stress; I bopped over to the closest electrician's booth and ordered $1,000 worth of lights. Ka-ching.

My style was very Marilyn Monroe at the time. I had short platinum-blonde hair, big red lips, and perky boobs. I wore vintage slips, and Beth dressed like a carnival queen. Our unique styles fit right in with Macbeth's eclectic vibe.

I'd say there were upward of forty thousand people in attendance. Stores from all over—everyone from Neiman Marcus to smaller boutiques. But all the buzz was focused on the newcomer, Macbeth Collection. Our merchandise was so adorable that we got about $60,000 worth of orders that day in one fell swoop. We suddenly realized, *Holy shit, we have a real business here*. Our thoughts then turned to panic. I was purchasing our buckets at retail from Home Depot. I flipped over the closest one to me and dialed the number on the bottom. I got ahold of the distributor in Texas and made a deal to purchase them at wholesale. Our kitchen couldn't sustain this company anymore—we needed to open a factory. There was no one to guide us. I had to think on my feet *fast* and learn on the go.

Jan already had a lace and embroidery factory, and seeing as the garment industry was on a downturn while my business was on an upswing, he offered for us to move into the unused space. We even took on some of Jan's employees with the deal. Things were growing at warp speed. We moved from using vintage wallpaper to designing our own patterns. We leased large printers so we could create the designs in bulk to meet the demands. We had all the materials on hand to fulfill orders quickly. We had quite the little operation going, but in order to keep it afloat we needed another cash infusion.

Jan was able to see our hard work in action and didn't consider Macbeth Collection to be a hobby anymore. He generously invested $35,000. Did he believe in me? In a half-assed way. It was my father-in-law who really believed in me. He told Jan, "It's a good idea. She knows what she's doing." He got me, because he was a serial entrepreneur. He had started businesses left and right, businesses that succeeded and businesses that failed. He founded Josephs Brothers Embroidery, which had brought great success to the entire family. One of the things I respected most about him was that he was never afraid of failure.

The irony is that once Jan had invested and his company was suffering, he decided it would be a great idea to go into business with me. Did he believe in Macbeth Collection the way I did? Not so much. He would always say, *You're terrific at making money, but you're better at spending it.* I think Jan saw an opportunity to jump the sinking ship that was the garment industry at that time. He came on board but never seemed too happy to be there. The success of the business in his eyes was strictly monetary. I enjoyed being creative, watching it grow, and filling a need in the market. I knew that if the business was fueled by passion, the money would come. There's no such thing as an overnight success.

Jan always acted like he was doing me a favor, which meant that I never felt like we were a team. I wished the investment he'd made in the company hadn't filled me with guilt and anxiety, but it had. Nothing was ever *ours*. It was always his. I had some weird beholden feeling to him, which is upsetting in hindsight. I don't have that relationship with Joe. Everything we do, we do together. It's not mine or his, it's ours. I think that's why we have such an amazing relationship. Unfortunately, I dealt with that dynamic with Jan for longer than I should have.

Jan started looking into the finances and decided Beth had to go. He sat me down and said, "Listen, Margaret, we're putting up all the money, and you're giving her 50 percent of the business. I know you guys started together, and I know she has sweat equity, but we have to buy her out." I mean, he had a point; we were literally putting in everything, including the building. Jan added, "Or she can buy you out and you start something else; it's one or the other. I'm not going into a business where I lay out everything and then give someone else half of it."

I felt physically ill. She either had to take less of a percentage or get up to speed on computer graphics, because that was the way the industry was going. Beth was more of a fine artist, and I realized we'd have to pay graphic designers if she couldn't adapt. I wanted to give her an opportunity to pick up the slack. Unfortunately, Beth did not like that idea. She was highly offended and took it personally that I thought the business was evolving beyond her skill set. *Maybe Jan had a point; she had to go.* I had my background from FIT and could operate as the creative director. I knew what the trends were. I knew what the styles were. And I knew monogramming was going to be the next big hit.

What ensued was a big fallout between us and the disintegration of our friendship. I explained to her: "We're putting a lot of money into it. It's much more lucrative for you to take a smaller slice of a big pie." But she was too angry to see that. So, ultimately, we signed an agreement and bought her out.

She hated my guts, and that was it. I was sad to lose a friend this way, but it was strictly a business decision. I remember she said to me, "I'll wave to you when you're on *Oprah*; you think you're so fucking great." Oprah's not on TV anymore, but I am. So hi, Beth.

After Beth and I parted ways, we took the business to a different level. I felt badly about cutting her out, but I don't think we could have grown to the level we did with her still on board.

The bottom line is that it's not a good idea to go into business with a good friend. I think you can become friends after you go into business together, but mixing money and friendship is just too complicated. Things go south very fucking quickly. I learned that lesson early on. Have I made the mistake again? Absolutely. By the way, Albert Einstein said that's the definition of insanity—to do the same thing over and over again and expect different results. I must be certifiably insane.

But I'm also a certifiable optimist. And why shouldn't I be? We created something out of nothing, which, in and of itself, was impressive. We took utilitarian items and made them stylish and fabulous—no one else was doing that. We also started doing monogramming before monogramming had made a comeback. Every competitor was watching us for the next move. It felt really great, even though I was constantly anxious. I was like, *Oh my God, where are my buckets? Is my shipment going to arrive in time?* I mean, we were importing entire containers from India. I was worried about when the checks were going to come in, when the products were going to come in. I was in charge of a factory, a team of employees, and quite a few showrooms. My plate was *full.*

Those were hard-core days. Regardless of all the stress they induced, I lived for them. It wasn't about the money. It was about the fun of going to the trade shows and being around other creative minds. It was the camaraderie of lifting other people up and watching them succeed. I savored every minute of it.

We could barely keep up with the demand for our storage line, but it's always important to keep coming up with fresh ideas as well. The next bestselling idea we came up with was our oversized custom clipboards. Every teacher at that time received one as a holiday gift, customized with their name. We were the first ones who ever did that. They were $12 wholesale and sold for $24 retail. Everybody loved them. We could not keep those clipboards in stock; it was actually entertaining. We would ship them wrapped in cellophane, topped with a bow, ready to be gifted. My neighbor actually came up with the idea; she worked for me part-time at the trade shows. When I told my father-in-law, he said, "Margaret, who's going to buy a clipboard for $12 wholesale?" Turns out everybody, that's who.

Though we weren't the largest company, we got endless press.

Our products were in "Oprah's Favorite Things" more than once. We were in *House Beautiful*, *Better Homes & Gardens*, and even *Vogue*. There wasn't a month that went by that we weren't featured in an article about hot gifts. Out of all the press, my most memorable accolade was when I was named *Country Living* Woman Entrepreneur of the Year in 2007. I was forty years old, had been in business eight years, and had really established myself in the industry at this point. It was a rewarding feeling to be acknowledged among my peers after so many years of hard work. All the other entrepreneurs and I flew out to Chicago for an inspiring weekend of camaraderie and celebration. It ignited my passion even more to uplift women in business. The following year I was invited to be on the panel to help choose the new entrepreneurs.

The one thing I will say is that starting your own business is not a guarantee. It's hard work. You never know which products are going to do well, and it's usually the opposite of what you expect. The things I thought were going to be big hits sometimes bombed. The advice I would give anybody looking to launch a company right now is *Learn from my mistakes*. Hire people who are good at something that you're not good at. I am fantastic at being a creative director and front person because I'm outgoing, confident, and creative, and can relate well to people. I suck at money, planning, and organization. So I always have someone who works with me who has the opposite skill set. This kind of balance is imperative to success. I would also advise you to do your research. First you have to come up with an idea. Hopefully it's unique and has not already been done before. If it has been done before, the goal is to improve upon what's out there. You're going to need some sort of a business plan; it doesn't have to be formal. If at first your finances are tight, there are many ways to work around that. You can offer your employees sweat equity in the business, but do it as a vesting option. When they hit certain bars of success and prove their worth, that's when they get more interest in the company. Don't go giving away equity freely. It's not a give-and-take until there is added value.

A lot of people say, *Trust your instincts*. But, honestly, my instincts were sometimes pretty shitty, especially when it came to picking partners. I would say talk to the smartest people you know who have been successful in business. Be a sponge; ask a lot of questions. Really listen, and do not think that you know it all. And finally—as I've already said—find a mentor. That's the most important thing. Don't ever feel threatened by other people's success. There's room for everybody to shine. Lift people up. I've been lifted up many times, and therefore it's essential for me to do the same for others. I believe that if you follow your passion and refuse to give up, you can make *anything* happen.

Life Lessons

- It's more important to know what you're *not* good at than what you're good at. Your strengths will always be there to play to, but your weaknesses could be the downfall of you.

- Surrounding yourself with successful people should inspire you, not make you feel inferior. Acknowledge that you've earned your seat at the table, then listen and learn.

- Being in business with friends can be great, if both friends mean business. Put *everything* in writing.

Chapter Nine

FAMILY AFFAIR

At first, I thought that working with my husband, my brother-in-law, and my father-in-law was going to be a business-savvy *Brady Bunch*. But instead, it was more like a twisted version of *The Golden Girls*. I was always dreading the inevitable need to ask Jan for more money. The main issue was that Jan and I had two totally different styles of working. He was very risk-averse, and I was very much so a risk-taker. You need to spend money to make money. As I always say, I'm 50 percent determined and 50 percent delusional. When I say delusional, it's not what you may think. It's more that I always believed that my dreams would become my reality from day one. I mean, if I don't believe my own hype, who will?

The thing is, Jan and his brother were not into the hype. They didn't understand the need to have a front person or a face of the brand. Not to mention that Macbeth was a start-up, and Jan and his brother's experience had been working in their father's lace and embroidery business, which was completely established and profitable by the time they got there. They never had to invest in the embroidery business like they did in mine. Even though we were doing well and garnering a lot of accolades, it still took money to keep things moving. I know that it was stressful for them to feel that they had to live off the same company they were financing.

Now, to me, of course, this wasn't stressful. It was motivation to hustle. I knew our kids' colleges were taken care of, we had savings, and this was the time to take a leap of faith. Macbeth Collection was operating on a new wave of doing business, and they just weren't into riding this wave. The days of cold calling, door to door, with your sample case in hand were gone; everything was moving in a digital direction, and it was a completely new culture to my family. Faxes were being replaced by emails, online retail orders were flooding in, and I was starting to be featured on blogs. I wanted to focus on things like PR and marketing so we could get our name out there even more and generate widespread interest in our brand. Jan and his brother would be very dismissive of ideas like these. It was more my brother-in-law than Jan. They looked at spending money on PR as a frivolous expense.

I think my natural public relations and marketing savvy must have come from the way I grew up. My mother always made the package look good. A company can say and sell whatever they want as long as there's a presentation and an image to accompany it.

Take the pet rock, for example. Someone had the wherewithal to know that putting a rock in a box would be lucrative. They sold out like crazy. I mean, they probably had little kids going into the fields and picking up rocks, and someone made millions and millions of dollars from that. Seriously, you can wrap shit in a pretty package and rake in the dough. Everything's about how you deliver it.

Gratefully, my father-in-law saw my magic and was supportive of taking the business to the next level. He invested personal money to pay for the PR. He was so accomplished himself that he wasn't fearful of taking business risks. He was a visionary and driven even at his age.

At this point, the company had branched out from just children's products into home accessories, pet products, stationery, and gifts. Macbeth was basically a complete lifestyle brand. I was the creative director and did all of the design with my team of graphic artists, while the rest of the family was concerned with the back end. They were in charge of shipping logistics, customer service, and vendor relationships at the thousands of shops we were selling to—the gamut ranged from small specialty boutiques to big-ticket stores like Neiman Marcus and Saks Fifth Avenue.

I always hoped for success but never imagined that it was going to reach the level that it has. It was like a ball that kept rolling and grew bigger and bigger. In hindsight, I probably should have changed the name of the business, since Beth was no longer a part of it. I thought about it when Beth left, but I felt that since we were getting so much press, it was too late. I did end up adding "by Margaret Josephs" to the name years later.

With my father-in-law's investments we hired a woman named Belle Courtney to take care of the company's PR. She really catapulted us into mainstream media. I loved her because her ideas were cost-effective. She would arrange private meetings with editors. Not only would she get us press for our products but she also branded me personally. She was able to see the importance of curating my face with the brand. This method blurred the lines between Macbeth Collection and Margaret Josephs; we were now one entity. While Jan didn't value PR, his ego loved to see us in the magazines—but of course, as per usual, it came down to *show me the money in the bank*. Many months, there was tons of money. Other months, we were reinvesting in the business and the bank account was lean. I was always working on proving myself in order to make Jan happy and proud. Thankfully, I don't feel like I have to prove myself to anyone anymore. I don't give a shit if people think my ideas are good or not. If I think something is a good idea, it is. Period. End of story.

At this time, we saw the need to hire a bookkeeper. Since it was a family affair and we were in need of another Golden Girl, Marge Sr. became available. She left her job at PepsiCo, took an early retirement package, and joined the team. In Marge Sr. fashion, she scored her own big office, leaving everyone else to share one. I'd constantly be screaming into her office, *Moooommm! Did you pay the fucking phone bills??* Human Resources would have maybe considered it unprofessional, but hey, *I was head of Human Resources*.

I could tell that the business as a whole was taxing for Jan's family. Meanwhile, Marge Sr. and I felt very differently. The entrepreneurial spirit was coursing through our veins. Jan, on the other hand, was starting to feel drained, emotionally and financially. Over the years, Jan had invested a lot of money in the company, and that half-million-dollar investment was weighing heavy on his mind. I knew we would make the money back. It's not like there wasn't going to be food on our table. But he who holds the gold makes the rules, which is the biggest lesson to learn.

It wasn't that I was irresponsible, I just knew how to compartmentalize. I had learned that from my mother. She was a little more delusional than I was. She never even thought to deal with tomorrow. I knew to deal with tomorrow, but I wasn't going to worry about it today. I had to live in the present and make it as fabulous as it could be. Jan could never enjoy the small wins, and the big wins were never enough for him. If I had a big win and was like, *Oh my God, we're getting a $90,000 order from this company out of Korea*, Jan would say, *I'll believe it when the money is in the bank.* And even once we *did* get the order and the money *was* in the bank, Jan would be like, *Okay, what's next?* That was very painful for me. His inability to appreciate those happy moments together put a strain on our marriage.

Jan and I were always known as the Bickersons in general, but once he joined the company, our fighting became exponentially worse. Jan liked to bring our work home, and I did not. Naturally, I liked talking about Macbeth—I lived and breathed it most of the time—but at the end of the day I didn't want to be peppered with hypothetical questions at the dinner table. Jan always obsessed over the what-ifs. Once I left the office, the only thing I was concerned with was spending quality time with the children as a family. I needed that time to rejuvenate. But the company was all-consuming to Jan. Things can consume me, but at the appropriate times.

I would literally take a picture frame off the wall and stab the photo of us together out of frustration. And then I would be able to walk out the front door with a smile, as if we hadn't just had the craziest fight. See, I'm not the easiest person to live with. I have a horrible temper and can viciously lash out. That being said, I'm very considerate. I don't like to suck the life out of a room. I'm a professional showgirl. I would show up at trade shows with my best face forward no matter what had happened an hour prior. I had to. That's business. You have to always bring your A game. I wasn't going to let Macbeth suffer because of my personal life.

Our constant fighting really bothered my brother-in-law, Kurt, which was part of why we didn't always see eye to eye. Kurt suggested I throw in the towel on numerous occasions—*Just close up the business, cut your losses, get a regular job*. I would get my point across—that that wasn't happening—through an unproductive screaming match. When he would get really frustrated, he would say to me, *Face it, you're never going to amount to anything.* And then I would reply with something vicious like, *Don't worry about me; you'll always be a never was.* I had been so stifled by men back in my younger years that I just couldn't stand to take it any longer. I was strong enough now to use my voice to defend my company and myself. Looking back, we said things just to hurt each other, and it upset me because I really did love him.

There were plenty of times when I felt that Kurt's unsolicited advice interfered in our marriage as well. He took it upon himself to tell us that we should sell our house in Tenafly and move to a cheaper town. He thought that would ease Jan's stress. Those were the types of things he shouldn't have gotten in the middle of. It was our marriage and our decision. It wasn't his place. There are some things that are said that you can't unhear, or ever forget.

Did Jan ever come to my defense? Of course not. I never felt very protected by my husband. Jan should have stepped in; Kurt and I should never have had to discuss those issues. Sadly, Jan didn't understand how to set proper boundaries, and when you work with family, you have to know how to put those in place. In fact, I'd say that in life in general there have to be defined limits. I'm well aware of this because my mother also had an issue with boundaries. She isn't my mother; she is my best friend. That's probably why I married someone with the same issues.

It was a very draining dynamic between Kurt and me because on one hand I loved him so much because he was the best uncle to my children, almost like a second father. He was smart, handsome, and charming. We had a special friendship where we could talk about anything; I would even be his plus-one to events when his wife couldn't attend. I think that's why it was so painful for me when we argued. I feel as though our relationship would never have gone so south if we hadn't gotten into business together. My spending habits should have been between me and Jan, not my entire family. It was like I had three husbands, my father-in-law included. There was a particular uproar when I spent $400 on new bras. The credit card bill came in, and I walked into the office to a half-hour debate on how much a bra *should* cost. Eventually I shut them up when I explained that it was cheaper than a tit-lift.

Even though Jan wanted to murder me half of the time, he still loved walking into a room with me on his arm. I was the life of every party even without drinking. It worked for Jan because he always had a driver. I would dance all night, and we would always be the last to leave. I was always the fun girl, and he found it infectious to be around me. I could make calm out of chaos and lemonade out of lemons. There would be these obligatory trips to the house of my in-laws' friends Libby and Arnold that were collectively dreaded by the family. But I would turn them into an event. Jan loved that I could bring the fun into every situation. Instead of complaining and focusing on the negative, I chose to find the joy in everything. I was the ultimate hype girl. It's innate for me to be that way, but at the same time it was exhausting and emotionally draining to feel responsible for changing Jan's mood. By the time we would leave Libby and Arnold's, he would say, *That was the greatest day all because of you. I don't know how you do it.* But as much as he loved that about me, sometimes he found my eternal optimism unbearable. Everything that he loves about me he also hates about me. We're just two very different people. I learned only after years of therapy that you can't be responsible for someone else's happiness. It comes from within.

You would think, because we worked together, our days would be identical. But even a typical workday was very different for each of us. Macbeth was everything, but it couldn't stop me from being a hands-on mom. I was always the first mom to volunteer for the school trips; there was no way I could take a chance on someone losing my precious cargo. Every morning I would stay back to take Cooper to school. For breakfast he would have homemade waffles and bacon served to him on a tray in bed while he consumed his favorite morning television. We would then hurry to school and manage to be consistently late by five minutes every day. Cooper's public school didn't have a cafeteria, so every day there would be a choice from three different local restaurants to deliver lunch. The thing is, Cooper didn't like those choices. So I would arrange for a fourth restaurant to deliver. The office staff became my best friends. After my grueling morning of scheduling takeout, I would arrive at the office around 10:30 a.m.; I would have been able to get there by 10, but I needed my morning Starbucks.

Here's a funny tangent about Starbucks. Years before Starbucks existed, I came home from a trip to New Orleans and told Jan I wanted to open a coffee bar. I thought New Jersey could benefit from a Café Du Monde. We all know my obsession with coffee started young. He said point-blank, "Margaret, who's going to pay $5 for a cup of coffee? That's absurd." A year later a Starbucks popped up around the corner from us. Clearly, I could spot a trend.

With my $5 coffee in hand, I would listen while Jan caught me up on what I'd missed. Jan would drive into the office at 8 a.m. and read his emails over a cup of *shitty* coffee. I would work with my creative team to come up with new ideas and concepts, get in touch with Belle to see what PR opportunities we had, then prep for the numerous trade shows that we did throughout the year. Jan would handle customer orders while sneaking looks at porn in between calls.

For lunch I would head to the back office and eat with my creative team, since Jan was all about tuna on a salad. He was neurotically healthy, unlike me, who loves a little fat with her meal. Jan is a little OCD with his routine. He would excessively floss his teeth post-lunch. He was a serial tooth flosser, and he didn't care who was watching. It wasn't uncommon for me to get a piece of his lunch flicked out of his teeth onto my face while discussing a shipment. Jan would explain, *If your gums aren't healthy, it could lead to a variety of diseases.* He spent 90 percent of his time preserving himself. After work, Jan would never come directly home. He'd go to the gym every single night, but first he'd have to take a nap in the gym parking lot to get his energy up. Don't think I know this because I was there with him. It was just the talk of the town, and I would get called constantly with reports of Jan passed out in his car. He was always in great shape, so I guess the naps worked.

I would go directly home and start organizing dinner with Inez, who was our live-in jack-of-all-trades. Not only did she take care of Cooper and the house, she was an *amazing* cook. She would always have to make two different dinners every evening because Cooper existed on filet mignon and homemade french fries, while Jan would never ever *think* of eating a steak (too much fat content); he was big into chicken.

Our life was very streamlined, but it was also crazy. Everything was to the extreme. We would be passionately affectionate and viciously hurtful to each other within the same minute. I knew that it wasn't *normal*, per se. I mean, is that how husbands and wives are supposed to act? A lot of it lay in the stress of being in business together. It's abnormal to spend twenty-four hours a day with anyone. Macbeth was my baby. I grew it from a little seedling. I created an industry. Jan just could not relate.

Though Jan and I fought like cats and dogs, we had a very big social life to attend to. Even though we were the Bickersons, there was a charm to us. Our fighting was more like sophisticated sarcasm. People found it to be like dinner and a show. Our social circle was vast and included the parents of Cooper's friends, whom I'd met at Temple Sinai. Twentysomething years later and they are still my closest friends. Our Fridays and Saturdays were booked months out. Sundays were off-limits and stayed reserved for our big family dinners.

Our chaotic lives came to a devastating halt when my father-in-law was diagnosed with non-Hodgkin's lymphoma. He fought for six years. It was completely earth-shattering to our family when he passed away. I felt like I'd lost my own father. He was the glue that held together the craziness. Our true patriarch. Our rock. It felt like the world had dropped out from under our family. My mother-in-law, Miriam, was the love of his life. They had been together since they were fourteen years old. Heartbroken could not even describe how she felt. She never truly recovered from his passing. They were your typical Jewish in-laws. He was very dapper—always with his hair slicked back, perfectly coiffed; a meticulous dresser, a fantastic dancer—and the most generous man I've ever known, in all aspects. Miriam had been a swimsuit model in her younger years. She had beautifully wavy hair and a gap between her front teeth, like Madonna. In her later years she looked like Endora from *Bewitched* with her fiery red hair and fake lashes. Always high glamour. Their only goal in life was to see their children and grandchildren happy.

I really had no idea what was going to happen once my father-in-law was gone. Who would I call when Jan and I had one of our knock-down, drag-out fights? Who would be my cheerleader? What would happen to Sunday nights? I knew that losing him would make or break our family. Everybody was either going to band together and be stronger for it or it was going to tear us apart. Unfortunately, it tore us apart.

Nothing felt stable anymore. There were many days I wasn't sure if things were going to work out in my marriage. I would convince myself that I was going to get through this and we were going to be happy. I wasn't going to get divorced, right? *I'm not going to be like my mother.* And there were other days when I was like, *Dear God, please send me someone else*. I mean, we would go to parties and every husband would be dancing with his wife. I would beg Jan and he would refuse, so I'd dance with everybody else's husband. I felt like he was handing me out on a silver platter and that he must be having the same internal thoughts too.

Do I think that being in business together for eleven years caused all our problems? *No*. But it put a spotlight on our already existing issues. It was the nail in our coffin.

A year or so after Jan's father passed, I was at the International Gift Show, and my good friend Polly from Oklahoma, who was also exhibiting at the show, introduced me to the young woman she had working with her. She was visiting from England and staying with her aunt in the city. I stared back at the taller, blonder, skinnier British version of me, Lexi. Polly thought we were so alike that we would hit it off. She obviously was right.

We had a temporary holiday kiosk at Grand Central Station for a total of five weeks. It was incredibly high traffic, and I needed someone capable to staff it. Immediately I thought of Lexi. I called her up and offered her the gig. I stuck her in the Grand Central Station booth to field the thousands of holiday shoppers. She fared well; I knew she was a keeper. Initially she was only visiting, but when I offered to move her into my rent-stabilized apartment in New York City, she was here to stay, and she's never left me since. Beyond a shadow of a doubt, Lexi is one of the greatest things that's ever happened to me.

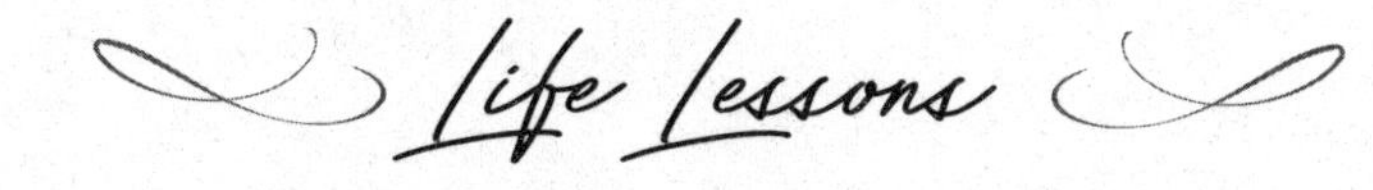

- Setting boundaries, in every aspect of your life, is the *most* important lesson I've learned. Especially with family.
- If you're in a business with family, it's more important to create a work/life separation than a work/life balance.
- Sidenote: Don't be afraid to take a refresher course on these two life lessons on a regular basis. I know I do.

Chapter Ten

BOOBS & BUCKETS

There would be no Macbeth without Jennine, and here's the crazy story of how I met her.

It was Christmastime, and my graphic artist Evan was complaining of a headache and blurry vision. Most of you would chalk that up to a migraine, but my hypochondria kicked in and I knew better. After a few days of obsessively reading through my medical books, I demanded that he go to the hospital. He explained that he couldn't because of a couple of reasons, the short list being that he was working for me part-time and didn't have health insurance. That's when I decided to rush him to Englewood Hospital, which I knew generously took charity cases. I just had a bad feeling. Hours later he was diagnosed with a brain tumor, and that night he was going to be transferred for brain surgery. I was a nervous wreck by his bedside, and then as they started to roll him away, I blurted out, "Hey, do you have someone you can recommend to cover for you?"

Okay, maybe I'm an asshole, but an asshole who saved his life.

Anyway, he recommended Jennine and I am forever grateful. Jennine really helped grow the company. She's an extremely talented graphic artist, a creative genius. She and I would brainstorm design ideas and then she would just pump them out. It was really something to watch. We would only argue over colors. But the two of us were in over our heads.

Three creative geniuses are better than two, so Lexi came and joined us full-time. Once Lexi had joined the business, I felt like I could finally take a breath. We were exactly alike, except she had no cellulite. Most important, we had identical mindsets—to make the company appear bigger than it actually was through great marketing and publicity. We were all about fun, fabulosity, and getting the job done—no matter what it took. So, it was seamless.

Lexi was also able to help me battle Jan, my brother-in-law, and anyone else who stood in my way. We'd hit the trade show circuit together and work as hard as we played. Like me, she wanted to put in the time, make money, and grow the business. We both had grand visions. Our motto was "Dream big, live big." I finally had a true partner in crime.

We're both extremely optimistic—the glass is always half-full. To this day, we never feel that we can't achieve something or can't get something done. We never had a deadline that we couldn't meet, even if by the skin of our teeth. The word "no" is simply not in our vocabulary. We don't ask *Why?* We ask *Why not?*

Lexi and I were two unstoppable blonde bombshells with big

boobs, out on the loose. People would come to the trade shows just to interact with us and see what we were wearing, which was always something over the top. Our head designer, Jennine, was the brownie to our blondies. The three of us were the ultimate "unprofessional showgirls," in our sequins and high heels everywhere we went. We were a triple threat. We had our boobs on display and our fake eyelashes fluttering. We looked like a rock-and-roll girl band—the kind you would want to take home, just not to your mother. Just so you know, I was younger, thinner, and tanner back then; after all, it was a lifetime ago . . . Well, it feels like it—it was 2008. We would show up and act like we owned the place, because we knew that in order to achieve something, it took one half skill and the other half attitude. If you look and act the part, people will believe in you. If you seem insecure and like you don't belong, you won't fit in. We were all about owning it.

The three of us were always prepared to flirt with anyone who could help us, including electricians, security guards, and parking attendants. We had our own set of rules. There were times when we were at the Javits Center and didn't want to pay for extra lighting but wanted the booth to be lit up like Las Vegas, so I'd say to Lexi, "Go flirt with Big Mike, the head electrician." I knew he had a thing for her. So, of course, we got whatever lighting we wanted for free. *Welcome to the Strip.* We weren't shy. We did what we had to do to get a discount. Nothing was beneath us when it came to bettering the business. (Now, in my personal life, I would never pull this shit. I'd be mortified.)

Jennine is an unbelievably talented artist, a creative genius, and funny in a Goldie Hawn way. She wasn't as tough as Lexi and me, though, and was a little bit of a chicken. We would tease her all the time to see how long it would take us to get her to cry. We sound like mean girls, but it was very sisterly and done with such deep love. Jennine and Lexi both lived in the city. They would commute to New Jersey together on the ferry, and I would pick them up, and the three of us would start our day over breakfast together. Sometimes we would work twenty-four-hour shifts to get the job done. All of my employees really became part of my family. I would take us on little vacations together, from New Orleans to Miami and even mini getaways to Atlantic City. I have the fondest memories of that time.

The mentality of the trade show was sell, sell, sell, no matter the circumstances. The show opened at 9 a.m., and we had somehow formed a weird superstition that if we didn't get our first order by 11 a.m. it was going to be a shit day. We would be frantically checking the time, in fear of 11 a.m. Then, like clockwork, by 10:55 a.m. we would have a line down the aisle.

It's almost impossible to paint a picture of just how crazy the gift industry was back then. Truthfully, the cast of characters were too creative to fit into the conventional corporate structure. We were a band of "real job" rejects. All bets were off; misbehaving was rampant, and code-of-conduct breaches were a daily occurrence. Not only were the vendors lunatics but the customers were certifiable. There was no social decorum; it was like banter at the bazaar. Insults were traded with affection and usually got you a bigger sale. If you wanted someone's attention, you would not hesitate to pull them by their arm into your booth, without even looking at their badge.

It could have been Bergdorf's or Bertha's Gift Shop from Bumfuck, and it didn't matter. Every order and every customer was important to us. As much as it was business, it was like a sport. The beauty of that was everyone had started their own company out of passion and love. Myself included. Now, *this* should have been a reality show.

Every night after the trade show we'd go out and celebrate our successful day. I always wanted to treat my staff to the most glamorous dinners in NYC after a hard day's work. If we were traveling, we would be out the whole damn night like it was a vacation, specifically when we traveled to Atlanta. In my opinion, Atlanta has the food and entertainment to rival New York City. We would frequent the gay bars and drag shows and end up onstage. In the early hours of the morning, we would head back to the hotel and nearly collapse. We would all share one room, but in the finest hotel, Lex and I in one bed and Jennine sprawled across the other. A few hours later the alarm would go off and we would all be dragging. The girls would need twenty-seven coffees to jolt them out of their hangovers and I would need twenty-seven to jolt me out of sleep. Then back to work we'd go.

Without a doubt Lexi became the sister I never had. We were both only children. Her parents were divorced as well. We had similar upbringings and felt that we were kindred spirits, destined to meet. We're both very maternal and nurturing to each other. We finish each other's sentences, like she's in my brain. She has become my biggest cheerleader and confidant. She's the only person I trust with everything, and I never have to second-guess her. We never fight or get upset with each other. I want everything great for her.

Whatever I have, I want her to have. I want to bring her up in this world. It's one of the best relationships in my entire life. We're totally inseparable.

We became so close that she practically lived in our house. She would sleep over most nights of the week. If I slept with Cooper, she would sleep in his bed too. If she and I were up late at night in my bed watching movies, Jan would just crawl in the bed and sleep with us. Not in a creepy way.

A lot of people were envious of our relationship. Not Jan, though. He loved Lexi. She was like his other daughter. Conversely, my mother was a little jealous at first, but now she lives for Lexi; they're even next-door neighbors. She's known as Grandma Margaret to Lexi's son, Nino. Joe gave Lexi away at her wedding; she's also like a second daughter to him. I don't know how Lexi could be my sister and Jan's or Joe's daughter. It's some crazy sister-wife thing, but it's fine. It works for us, and Lexi will always be a part of my family. We're all so blessed to have her. I hope to buy her a house one day, because she truly deserves everything amazing in this world. You know, sometimes I think that Lexi was sent to me from up above by my father-in-law and my grandparents. I believe that they knew I had too much on my plate and said to themselves, *We have to give her Lexi. How can she do it without someone right next to her?*

Jennine and Lexi were privy to the issues I was having with Jan. It was hard to keep things private when we would have screaming matches in the office. They would get into it with him as well. Jennine would cry sometimes from the fights Jan and I would have, and I would do a lot of crying in the back of our office, saying things like, *This isn't the life that I want. I can't live like this.* Jennine and Lexi would give me pep talks, and I would pull through, but that didn't make it any less painful. It could be a full-on war at the office but we always put down our weapons for dinner. You know nothing can get between me and a meal.

I remember one specific instance that was very poignant and really changed everything for me. Our son Cooper has horrible, life-threatening food allergies. While Jan and I were at work, Cooper was at a friend's house and ate a piece of pound cake, which he didn't realize had almonds in it. He didn't have his EpiPen with him and, therefore, had to be rushed to the emergency room. Hospital trips were very frequent in my family—thank God we lived right around the corner.

Now, you'd think we'd both rush out of work to be at Cooper's side, right? *Nope.* Jan thought one parent was enough. In my momentary panic I couldn't find my car keys, and Jan refused to lend me his car. As I mentioned earlier, losing the car keys was a trigger for him to start fighting. He actually said to me, "You're not leaving until you find your own keys." I was literally on my knees crying and begging. *Please, just let me take your car. Please, I'll do anything.* He didn't give a shit. It seemed that it was more important to him that we find the keys than that I get to our son. In his mind, Cooper was in the hospital getting treated, so he was fine. In my mind I was like, *What the fuck are you talking about? He's our child. He needs us.* My son is everything to me, and to Jan too. Yet he couldn't see past how he was going to get to the gym after work without his car. OCD at its finest.

Thank God my mother was there. In the midst of all of this, I yelled to her, "Go, go, go!" I was desperate, and gratefully we were on the same page. She immediately left for the hospital in her car. In retrospect, I should have gone with her, but I was fighting with Jan and grabbing all my stuff, so I sent her running as soon as the call came in. In our true sorority form, Jennine and Lexi tackled Jan to the floor and forced him to give me the keys to his car. It was not a pleasant scene, but I didn't care. My sole focus was on getting to Cooper as quickly as humanly possible.

It was 2009, and the swine flu pandemic was in full force, so the hospital was overflowing with patients. Cooper was out in the hallway. He'd just arrived and was throwing up. Thankfully they recognized that he was going into anaphylactic shock and administered the EpiPen in time. Jan then decided to show up a bit later and was like, *Oh, he seems fine. I'm going to the gym.* He left me and my mother alone with Cooper, and in that moment, I said to myself, *I'm done.* It's not that Jan was a bad person. He just didn't have the emotional capacity that I needed in a partner. I had the extra emotional capacity for both of us for many years, but at this point it had worn thin.

In 2009 it also came time to plan Cooper's Bar Mitzvah, and Jan made everything as difficult as it could possibly be. Growing up, I never knew what Bar and Bat Mitzvahs were. I was Catholic and we didn't live in a town with many Jewish people, but as a mother to Jewish children, I was a fast learner. Every weekend during Bar/Bat Mitzvah season we had two or three extravaganzas to attend. I went to fifty-two Bar and Bat Mitzvahs, and Cooper attended well over a hundred, no exaggeration.

Since Cooper was one of the youngest in his grade, his Bar Mitzvah ended up being the last of the year, so I'd had the opportunity to see what everyone else had done firsthand. Lexi, Jennine, and I could not wait to plan the event of the century. Of course, in classic Jan fashion, he didn't want to have an over-the-top celebration. He felt like he had done it already with the older children and was over it. There was so much arguing back and forth about the budget that Jan and I actually went to therapy to work it out. The therapist literally had to say to Jan, "Why are you trying to deny your third son what the others had?" By the time he finally signed off on it, we had about twelve weeks to execute.

We no longer belonged to the temple, since Jan felt that being Jewish was more cultural than religious. That was fine with me, considering I never converted. So we opted for a more cultural event and deemed it a Faux Mitzvah. I planned tirelessly with the girls and even created a custom logo of a black skull with drumsticks, since Cooper is a drummer. It was a rock-and-roll-themed white party that took place on a New York City rooftop in June. There was a DJ and live musicians. I was dressed in a stunning white MoMo FaLana dress with a pale lilac tie-dyed tulle underskirt. Our family was all color-coordinated in white with hints of lilac. Jan gave a beautiful speech and thanked me for planning such a magnificent party. We danced until the wee hours of the morning. Cooper performed a drum solo and then dove into the crowd like the true rock star that he was that night. I still look at the pictures and consider it one of the best nights of our family's lives. I can't believe I was able to pull it off, knowing what was going on behind the scenes.

The whole affair ended up coming close to $100,000. Jan thought it was decadent and crazy, but I just couldn't put a price on our memories. When it was coming down to the wire, Jan was pissed at how over budget we were. It pushed him over the edge, and he told me, "I'm not footing the bill for the rest of it. I don't care how you pay for it." That was his typical thing—*find the money*. Unfortunately, that always presented a challenge because I didn't have a lot of access to our finances. I thought he was being completely ridiculous, but he was adamant. He told me, *I don't give a shit*. Final word.

I threatened to sell my engagement ring to cover the last of the costs. How do you think he responded? He said, "Go the fuck ahead." I was so disgusted with him; I thought he would say, *Don't be ridiculous*. Although maybe I shouldn't have been surprised. He was always one to call my bluff. It was a defining moment; I think then and there we both thought our marriage was through. But I couldn't dwell on that; I had a party to throw, so I sold my engagement ring *and* I threw my diamond wedding ring in too.

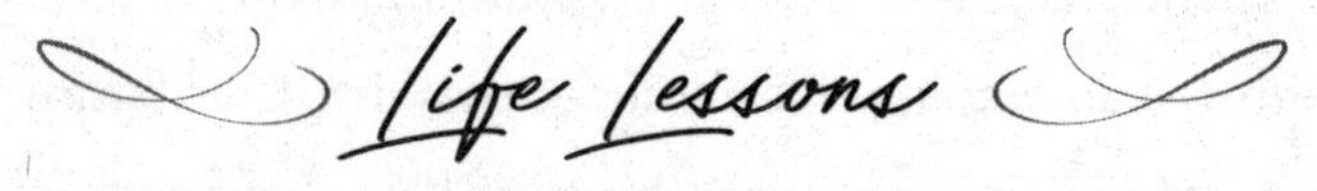

- If you don't believe your own hype, no one else will.
- I don't see roadblocks—I just see speed bumps and an opportunity to reroute. Ask all questions, exhaust all avenues, and eventually you'll get to the destination.

Chapter Eleven

FIXING THE PIPES

After the Faux Mitzvah, Jan and I were not in a good place. I was holding on to hope that things would get better, even though I knew in my heart that they probably wouldn't. We had been together for a long time—eighteen years, fifteen of those married. I felt like we were so far gone that we just couldn't get it back.

From the outside everything looked fine. We were still doing things as a family, going to events together, and even having sex. It's just that the love spark and respect were gone. We were going through the motions. We loved each other as family but not the way a husband and wife should. He'll say I was checked out, although I believe that, mentally, neither of us was there.

Everything doesn't have to be about me. I'm not a needy person, but I wanted someone who could focus and live in the now rather than be preoccupied with all the minutiae. We simply were not in the same place in life, and it had nothing whatsoever to do with the fact that he was much older than I was. Many people thought it was the twenty-year age gap, but that was the least of our issues.

I still found Jan attractive physically. It was just that, emotionally, we were no longer on the same page. Most of the kids were out of the house. Cooper was older. Everything had just fallen by the wayside, and I knew I needed to figure out what I was going to do with my life, beyond Jan. Jan and I were in couples and family counseling to try to salvage what was left of our relationship, but it wasn't working. I was doing anything to keep myself distracted from what was really going on in my life. I started going out a lot more without Jan. I was always big into going to concerts: Aerosmith, Bon Jovi, and my favorite band from high school, Foreigner. Foreigner was on tour that year, and I must have gone to six of their concerts, always front row. I actually took Jan to the first one with me, but once I locked eyes in person with the gorgeous lead singer, Kelly Hansen, I had this weird feeling that I needed to go alone to the next one.

After a year of hot-blooded tour chasing, my friends and I conveniently found ourselves in the same bar as Kelly after a show in Red Bank, New Jersey. He summoned us over to his table. Next thing I knew, he was telling me that he had noticed me in the crowd over the past year. I got shy and left, thinking, *What the fuck am I doing?*

Then I was like, *I can't miss this opportunity*. So, as I was driving, I called the Molly Pitcher Inn, the best hotel in Red Bank, and asked for Kelly Hansen's room on a whim. Lo and behold, they connected me. To my luck the phone rang and no one picked up. So I left a message. Something along the lines of *If you want to see me again, I'll meet you tomorrow after your concert on Long Island.* Then . . . my phone died. I got home and plugged it in and there was a voicemail waiting for me—*Come back! I fly out tomorrow night on the red-eye.* I was going to miss my opportunity after all, but then it dawned on me . . . I had his cell phone number.

Two months go by. I see that Foreigner is going to be on *The Today Show*. So naturally I text Kelly. He immediately texts back with his travel plans and tells me to meet him for dinner that night in the city. This time I was *not* going to miss my opportunity. I tell Lexi and Jennine to cover for me as I run out of the office. I go immediately for a bikini wax and to buy a new outfit.

I drive to the city, a mix of nerves, excitement, and anxiety. I wasn't thinking clearly, *obviously*. He was waiting outside the restaurant when I got there. His long hair definitely looked better than mine. Yes, I was wearing pigtails. We laughed when we saw each other, as he told me he wasn't sure if I was going to show because he thought I might have been drunk when I texted him. Little did he know I don't even drink. We had a great dinner, but we both knew where the night was going. He invited me up to his conveniently close hotel room, where I had to be snuck in past his bandmates.

It's always very awkward to have sex with someone you barely know. Even if you've been completely obsessed with them from afar. The only thing I remember from the heated experience is his ass being smaller than mine and his long, flowy hair strewn over the pillows as I sat on top of him. Before I left, he told me, "You know I have a girlfriend; don't tell anyone." I said, "Don't worry, I have a husband."

Back to my reality . . . Jan and I were still going to therapy, yet there wasn't much progress being made. There were too many moving parts. Everything was so intertwined—work, family, the kids. I had more people to think about than just myself. It was all falling apart, and it was getting harder and harder to be the person holding it all together. I felt guilty because I didn't want to hurt anyone, and I felt responsible for breaking up my family unit. It was weighing so heavily on me that I would get physically ill. On the outside, all the components for my dream life were there, but I couldn't pretend that it was working any longer. Three of my children were out of the house, grown adults, living their own lives. Cooper was still at home but busy with high school and the social life that comes with it. It was glaringly obvious: When Jan and I were alone in the house together, we couldn't keep up the charade.

Still, Jan's biggest concern was not our marriage but our finances, in my eyes. In his eyes, he felt that if our finances were perfect, then our marriage would be fixed. Of course, money in the bank does not equal a happy marriage. Unfortunately, Jan is like a furnace, and a furnace is never full. His overriding issue was that I always spent too much. It didn't matter what I was spending on, whether it be groceries, household items, or clothing, it was always too much. I am known to be a decadent spender, but I was also a major contributor to the family—not only financially but, more important, as a mother to our children.

The psychology behind people's relationship with money is very interesting to me. It's the main source of marital issues. Jan's parents were successful and able to provide him with a comfortable upbringing. That being said, I think he focused too much on comparing himself to others. I never walk into a room and assess what everyone else has. A compare-and-despair attitude is one I could never relate to. We were wealthy in relation to most people in the country, but there will always be someone wealthier and more successful than you. That should not make you feel less than.

I feel very accomplished to have started something from scratch and turned it into a major lifestyle brand. I always worked on my own and did everything for myself. And I received a lot of accolades for it. With that said, I never believed that my success was defined by my bank account. It was defined by my ability to choose happiness. I know that I'll always be able to support myself and carry on, because I have a strong sense of self.

Jan isn't wired the way I am. He can't comprehend my ability to be optimistic in the face of adversity. That doesn't make either of us right or wrong, it just makes us different, and not the best match. He often says to me, *If I were you, I'd probably have a nervous breakdown and blow my brains out*, and I just crack up. He sees how much pressure there is on me to take care of a lot of people. There's always something chaotic going on, but I was raised in chaos, so it's nothing new to me. I've had to deal with health issues with our son, lawsuits, bad partners in business, great financial loss, and betrayals from my dearest friends. And yet I keep going with a smile on my face and the faith that everything will be better than okay, it will be magnificent. I'll make sure of it.

As I've said before, there's no reward without risk. Whether it's in business or in your personal life, you must take a leap of faith toward your true goals. There are no guarantees in life. Things can change on a dime. The one sure bet is yourself. People don't realize that. The rewards of making tough decisions for yourself—the sense of achievement and security—are priceless. They afford you the self-confidence to know that you can accomplish anything you put your mind to.

I think that's why I was ultimately able to leave Jan. Believe me, it wasn't easy. No one wants to break apart a family, especially not one as close as ours. There were many sleepless nights when I lay awake agonizing over it. My family was and still is the most important thing to me. The thought of not being with my children, even though most of them were grown adults and living their own lives, was extremely painful. How could I not be with them every Sunday night for family dinner? I mean, in my head, I had Pollyanna vibes. I was like, *Even if Jan and I get divorced, we'll still be together every Sunday. If Jan gets a girlfriend, she'll join us.* Wishful thinking, but we weren't there yet. In fact, Jan and I were planning a fabulous family vacation back to Anguilla, where we had had our honeymoon. I think it was a last-ditch attempt to make things work between us.

Anyway, despite the situation with Jan, I had no idea that the love of my life was about to be delivered to my doorstep. Jan and I were in the process of doing a little home renovation, and my interior designer Marco hired this contractor, Joe, to come over and install built-ins around the house and put in the molding.

I wasn't actively open to meeting someone else, but apparently I was actively open to considering ending my marriage. I knew things weren't good, and I knew it was a matter of time until things were completely over. I just didn't know when or how. I didn't know if it was going to happen that year or three years down the road. But I was certain that Jan and I were not going to last forever.

That's when Joe walked into my house—with a plunger in his hand and a pipe in his pants. He recounts the moment I ran down the stairs in my wife-beater, pajama bottoms, and pigtails, braless with my bouncing boobs. I think that's kind of funny, because it's everyday Marge. It sounds like the perfect opening for a porn movie, but it's literally the way I come down in the morning. We had actually crossed paths before at numerous parties over the years at Marco's place, where he hosted with his partner, Chris. I remembered Joe, and he *definitely* remembered me. I would talk to Joe at those parties because his wife was never there. I won't mention exactly why she didn't attend, but let's just say she's very antisocial.

Joe had a great smile and was very charming, although I never thought twice about him as more than an acquaintance. As it turns out, he actually did think twice about me. He says that he was always smitten with me and thought I was beautiful and funny. Apparently, he brought me up to Marco more than once. He even said that at one particular party he was annoyed with Jan and found him adversarial. Still, we hadn't seen each other for years. Joe is horrific with names, so when he came to my house with Marco, he didn't realize whose home he was going to. He was pleasantly surprised when I bounced down the stairs. Marco said in his thick Venezuelan accent, "Oh, you remember Zhoe?" I did remember and thought he was adorable, but listen, he was a little outdated. He didn't have the goatee he has now, though he did have the most twinkly eyes and a beautiful smile, and he was very manly, with his clipboard ready to take instructions.

There was an instant flirtation, and I didn't mind that he was going to be in my house daily, working on my home that needed as much work as my marriage. To be clear, I wasn't like, *Oh my God, I'm going to bang this guy*. It was nothing remotely like that. We would have coffee together in the mornings before I would go to the office. Sometimes Inez would make us her famous homemade donuts, or I'd toast a French baguette to split. It was nice to have someone who seemed interested in me. We'd talk about everything and anything. We'd have these really deep conversations. Joe and I became instant best friends. The irony is that Jan even got to like him after a while.

After about three or four months on the job, I started confiding in Joe about my issues with Jan. It wasn't something I would have done right away, but ultimately we were very close, and I looked forward to him coming in every day. Amazingly, Jan didn't sense anything, even though there was major chemistry between us. I was starting to worry about it, like, *Oh my God, I'm very into this guy, something crazy is going on*. And Marco would tell me that Joe had a crush on me. Then, one day, Jan said, "Joe should be building our booths for the trade shows. He should travel with you." I thought, *Great*. I took Joe to lunch at Balthazar in the city to ask him to work for us at the trade shows. What better way to discuss business than over a glamorous meal? This was the beginning of the end. Jan basically handed me to Joe on a silver platter with a side of *pomme frites*.

Even looking back on that lunch now, I still get the same butterfly feeling in my stomach. I remember Joe must have been nervous too, because it was 11:55 a.m. and he ordered a seven and seven. As I've said before, he was a little outdated. He didn't get out much. (Thankfully, now he's upgraded to botanical gin.) He ordered a burger and I ordered steak frites. I even remember what I was wearing that day—flared jeans, Missoni clogs, and a floral fitted Western shirt, half-buttoned, with my boobs out. I no longer fit into that shirt, but I still have it hanging in my closet. I can't part with it. We lingered and laughed, and of course, he agreed to build the booths. Back to reality, I lost track of time and had to run to school pickup. It was raining, and as I teetered over the cobblestones in my clogs, Joe grabbed my waist tight so as not to let me fall. We both say the electricity was magnetic. No kiss, no funny business, but we knew.

Jan never thought I would want to be with a guy like Joe. He assumed if I was leaving him for anyone, it would be by private plane or yacht, for a real Wall Street type. Not for someone on a Harley carrying a wrench. He didn't realize how attractive someone like Joe could be to me. He was manly, nurturing, smart, caring, and confident in his being. He could walk into any room and not care who was there. He could talk to anybody and wasn't counting everybody's money. Those qualities are very attractive to me. Joe also didn't mind putting me on a pedestal; he didn't feel like he had to knock someone else down in order to build himself up. Those are the traits that make a man great.

Still, things didn't happen immediately between us. This was definitely a slow burn. The next time we saw each other outside of work was weeks later. He was going out of town on a motorcycle trip, and I had to go over scheduling with him before he left. I had a girls' dinner so I stopped into a local bar to meet him first. There was a Mets game on, and unbeknownst to me at the time, Joe is a die-hard Mets fan. When I saw him across the room, he was wearing what looked to me like a sporty dress. I realized it was actually a Mets jersey, but it looked like a dress on him. We all know Joe's not the tallest. I was like, *Oy! This needs work, but he is so damn cute.* It cemented how crazy I was for him because I didn't run out of there after seeing him in his dress over jeans. I couldn't fix the Mets jersey *that* night, but I did make a suggestion that he grow a goatee to accompany his mustache, which of course he did right away.

Jan and I weren't the only marriage in trouble. Joe shared with me that he and his wife were also very unhappy. They were sleeping in separate bedrooms and had been miserable for many years. Before they split up, he wanted his kids to be in college, which they were by this point. Like me, he was also torn about splitting up his family. This was all around the time of his wife's birthday, and lucky for me she didn't want to be with him to celebrate. Instead, he sent her away on vacation with a girlfriend. Conveniently, that left an opening for us.

There's a common misconception that Joe and I acted on our feelings when we first met, or within the first few weeks, but that wasn't the case. There was no impulsivity; we were slowly falling in love over many months and figuring out how to deal with it. It was agonizing but also insanely romantic. Leaving your husband for the contractor sounds like the stuff raunchy movies are made of, but we actually were two people who became best friends and gradually fell in love. If you can believe it, the first time we had sex was also the first time we ever kissed.

There was planning that went into our first time together. We had both put a lot of thought into our relationship and what it meant if we were going to act on it. We came to the conclusion that we had to be together. Joe booked a room at the Short Hills Hilton—he knew there could be no motels for The Marge. As we drove there in his Mini Cooper, which he still has, he kissed my hand incessantly. We needed an early check-in, so I told the front desk that I was sick and needed to lie down right away. They obliged. Though for some reason I think they knew what was going on . . . We didn't have any luggage.

When I got undressed, I had to forewarn him about my cheeseburger areolas. Luckily, cheeseburgers are his favorite meal. This might be TMI, but I couldn't believe someone in his fifties knew to manscape his crotch! I asked him, "How did you know to do that?" He told me that he read up in *Cosmo* beforehand—classic. Another important thing to mention, he has beautiful feet. I *hate*, and I mean *HATE*, ugly ungroomed feet on men. *This* could have been the deal breaker. Needless to say, the sex was amazing. After, we had naked room service, my favorite thing, and more sex. Then he had to shower because he told me my perfume was too strong and he was afraid his kids would smell it on him.

As we drove home, we both said, *Now what?* We knew that we were past the point of no return. We knew from that day on that we would spend the rest of our lives together. We just didn't know how we were going to get from point A to point B.

The rendezvous continued, but we upgraded to the Bowery Hotel in the city. It's still a special place for us. We go back and stay on Valentine's Day and birthdays. Joe loves a swanky hotel, fancy sheets, and great meals just like I do. But outside of our little hotel bubble, there were spouses and kids to think of. Lexi, Jennine, and Inez, our housekeeper, all knew what was going on. Inez ended up betraying me in many ways that I won't go into.

But I will go into this . . . Inez turned out to be *Single White Female*–ing me. Unbeknownst to me, she coveted everything I had. My clothes, my scent, my husband, and *my vibrator*! One payday I went into Inez's room to drop her payment in her nightstand drawer and there it was! My pocket rocket that had gone missing. Yes, I *know* it was mine. Also in the drawer, a stack of extra T-shirts from Cooper's Faux Mitzvah that I had been asking her about for the last five months—and to top it all off, multiple sticks of my vanilla-scented deodorant. *What a creep*. I immediately called my therapist, then Joe. As mentioned, Inez, although a creep, makes a fabulous donut. Joe was on the fence about whether or not to write her off completely; imagining a life without those donuts was hard to grapple with. In the end, *fuck the donuts*—she had to go.

Back to the affair: I wasn't discreet enough. I had told many of my girlfriends. I was worried that it would get back to Jan, but at the same time I think I wanted to get caught. Maybe I wanted Jan to fight for me as hard as I had fought for us. I fought hard for years for our family, but all I wanted was for him to show up for me. The problem was that Jan didn't think enough was wrong to even suspect that I would be looking outside of our marriage. Certainly prior to sleeping with Joe, I thought there was a possibility that my marriage to Jan could be saved, but eventually we were too far gone.

The thing was, even though my personal life was in turmoil, my business was really thriving. We were starting to do licensing, which was a huge expansion. More about that later. My world was such a whirlwind. It's hard to even remember everything that was going on. I wanted Joe and myself to unwind our marriages so that we could be together. We just couldn't figure out the right way to do it without hurting everyone we loved. It definitely went on too long before we planned on moving out of our respective homes.

I had a lot of anxiety about how things would play out. Although I never had any doubts about Joe. I like to say that I manifested him. I truly believe that. At night I would pray to God that my situation would change. When Jan and I went to parties, I'd be envious watching other couples. I would literally say, *Dear God, please let my next relationship be with someone who looks at me with love, who is nurturing, smart, funny, manly, capable, secure, kind.* Oddly, it got more specific; I wanted the type of guy who drove a motorcycle and had tattoos. Joe had every single quality except a tattoo . . . and now he has two.

We went together to a tattoo parlor, and we knew exactly what his tattoo would read. He got *Love the blonde you're with* on his arm. Obviously, I'm the blonde and will forever be his blonde—so I got a matching one that reads *The Blonde* on my wrist. This was my third tattoo. We did this the day before we moved in together, since a tattoo was the only thing he lacked on my manifestation list. Once we were married, Joe got *6.19.13*, our wedding date, tattooed on his ring finger. I got *The Mrs.* above the matching date on my arm, because he loves to refer to me as The Mrs.

I'd eventually gained the courage to tell Jan about my affair with Joe, in the safety of my therapist's office. I discussed this privately with my therapist for a very long time beforehand. I was trying to gain the strength and courage to do something that I knew would hurt someone I love so much. Suspicion was rising; my brother-in-law had confronted me because he'd heard from people in our town. My best friend Dawn also knew and was growing more concerned that Jan was going to hear it from someone else. Dawn and her husband were our closest couple friends since Jan and I had been together. Dawn and I were friends from our single days, but once I crossed the bridge to Jersey I made sure she did too. I didn't keep the affair from Jan to hurt him; it was just so much to grapple with, the idea of losing the life I had lived for twenty years. This was the only family I had ever known. This is not a justification or an excuse, and looking back I wish I had handled it differently.

I wanted to make sure that everything would be in order with my business before I blew the lid off things. I knew the divorce would not be smooth. I knew Jan would be very unhappy, and I was frightened that he would make things difficult for me. I had to figure out who was going to be bought out of Macbeth, and also how to be financially secure enough that I could walk out that door with the knowledge that our family would be okay. I wasn't going to put myself or my family in a position where the ducks weren't in a row.

I was shaking and crying the day I told Jan. As we sat in front of my therapist and the words left my mouth—*I'm having an affair*—it all became very real. All I could think about was the repercussions of the statement that I'd just made. He was calm, no tears. I was prepared for a big blowout and was shocked that he appeared stoic. I was a mess. Even after Jan knew that my affair was with Joe, he didn't ask me to leave. He wanted me to leave Joe and for us to work out our marriage. Sure, he was hurt. He was mad. But mostly he was shocked that it was Joe, of all people. We left therapy together and walked down the block for a sit-down Italian dinner. I cried over my spaghetti limone while Jan told me that it was all my fault between bites of his chicken paillard.

Jan was just very surprised by the whole thing. In his mind Macbeth was doing great, and he wasn't as stressed about money because of it; he assumed since the money was good then our issues could be worked out. He knew I was a flirtatious girl, but Jan was also a flirtatious man. We always knew we were going home with each other at the end of the night, though it didn't stop him from looking at everybody else. He definitely had wandering eyes. Obviously, I did too. Marriage is complicated and you can only judge your own. No one leaves a happy marriage. Fact.

Do I think Jan wanted me to stay because he was in love with me? *Not necessarily.* I think he didn't want to lose me because we had an amazing family. I can say that, to this day, I miss our family life beyond words. We had the most phenomenal times when we were together. There wasn't a dull moment; we were always laughing, crying, dancing, blasting music, and making every moment count. We were just so affectionate; we loved hard and fought hard. Our family was beautiful inside and out.

I was never allowed to be in a bad mood, because if I was off, then something must be really wrong. If there was a shift in my mood, it affected the whole. Jan would be worried. My kids would be worried. Honestly, it was so rare that I wasn't smiling, laughing, or in a naturally bubbly state. So when our marriage was shitty and I was starting to crack, everybody felt it.

It really rocked our family. The funny thing is, for as much as Jan didn't want me to leave, he didn't do much to get me to stay. He didn't try to turn it around. He wanted to keep me, but he didn't know how. He didn't pull out any stops, though if he had, I don't think I would have reconsidered. I was done. Either way, it would have been nice if he'd fought for me. There wasn't ever even a confrontation between the two of them, and Joe even continued to work for us!

It was the summer of 2011, and Jan had just been bought out of the business by one of my licensees for a generous sum. He gave up his 50 percent interest and I retained mine. More on this later. I was moving into a beach house down the shore in Mantoloking with Joe for the summer. Jan and I discussed in therapy that I would leave for the summer and he would look for a place to move into in September. We decided together with the therapist that it would be better for Cooper to stay in the marital home with his mother. That never happened.

We had the pressure weighing heavy of letting our four children know that we were getting separated. Cooper was leaving for a summer program, and we felt that we had to do it before he left. Jan and I sat them all down together to explain what was happening. Naturally, they were all devastated. Everyone cried. I didn't say I was going to be living with Joe for the summer, though I did say that I would be living down the shore. It would have been too much at once for them to hear, and would have made an already difficult situation much worse. We felt that the intimate details of our marriage should remain between the two of us. Unfortunately, due to my indiscretion, the children later became aware of the affair.

Never in a million years did I ever think that this would cause me to be estranged from two of my children. I was the only real mother they ever knew. I would *never* abandon them. I understood that there would be feelings of anger and pain, but in my mind, nothing could sever our bond.

That summer Lexi and I operated Macbeth from the beach house. My housekeeper, Inez, was with us, and Marge Sr. would come down for weekends. She was understanding of our separation. She knew our relationship was tumultuous and she wanted me to be happy. She was witness to years of turbulence that no mother would want to see her daughter endure. Her heart just broke for the kids.

Overall, the summer was a welcome escape. It gave me time alone with Joe that we had never been able to have before. But there were many tough days for me, particularly the Fourth of July. Traditionally Jan and I would have been at the beach in the Hamptons with our kids and his brother's family. It was hard to think that this was the first family tradition that was changing.

Joe understood perfectly; he was so comforting and sweet about it. Still, I cried the entire weekend. It wasn't that I wanted to be with Jan; it was that I was mourning the family dynamic that we no longer had. Joe didn't have the same struggle. When Joe told his children about us, they adjusted much easier. His relationship with his wife was also different. Joe was very close to his children but had been distant from his wife for years. Even though Jan and I had the tumult, there was such a deep emotional connection.

Joe's divorce was final before mine, and—in fact—he got off the hook easily because his wife served him with papers before he got the chance to break the news to her. She wanted him out and thought he would be devastated. When she found out that he was less than devastated and involved with me, she changed her tune. She called me up spewing insults, not only about me but the children as well. Listen, you can say whatever you want about me, call me a whore, a homewrecker, but you cross a line when you bring up something about my children. I cannot bear to write the horrible things she said to me that day. Unlike Jan and I, who remained extremely close, she and Joe do not have an amicable relationship. It must be painful to see the husband you couldn't stomach go on to be happily married on your TV screen every week.

When Jan and I separated, the kids didn't know about the affair. There was no reason for them to know the intimate details at the time. Joe was a catalyst, but Jan and I would have gotten divorced regardless. Since finding out about the affair, two of my older children have told me that it wasn't the fact that I was leaving their father but the affair itself that hurt them the most. They felt that it was a public embarrassment and disrespectful to their father. They're not wrong about that. But I will also say that in our town many men that my children know and respect have had affairs and have been given a free pass. I guess it's a different story if you stay in the marriage . . . you don't upset the apple cart. Personally, I think it's worse to live a lie.

To this day I'm not sure how my kids found out all the dirty details of my affair, but they know so much that it had to be from someone very close to me. Remember what I said about boundaries? It was my fault for not setting them; it was their fault for hurting my children. Regardless of who told them, it wasn't in the kids' best interest. They may have been trying to hurt me, but they hurt everyone in the long run. My estrangement from my two kids hurts me to my core, but it's also a loss for them.

I'll never forget the day I was at the beach with Dawn and her husband in the Hamptons, and they sat me down so her husband could lecture me on what a piece of shit I was. They questioned my parenting. They said, *You're going to wind up alone, and no one's going to talk to you. We're watching you drive a train into a wall.* Her husband also accused me of having Dawn lie to him about the $8,000 that she had lent me.

I never asked Dawn to hide it from her husband. I also had borrowed the money at a very low point in my life when I had no access to our funds. At that moment I really felt like I couldn't count on anybody; everything was constantly being thrown up in my face. I couldn't understand how my biggest confidant, a friend of twenty-three years, could turn on me like this. We were so intimate that I would pluck ingrown hairs out of her butt crack. I'm not kidding! I was the maid of honor in her wedding and the godmother to her daughter. It should also be noted that I repaid them. Cooper was heading to the Hamptons one weekend, and I sent him off with a check, saying, "When you see Dawn, give her this from me."

I believe that she was more concerned with how my divorce was going to affect her than me. No more family vacations together, no more summers together in the Hamptons. How was she going to keep her relationship with my brother-in-law and sister-in-law down the block from her in the Hamptons if her best friend was divorcing their brother? She didn't want to deal with awkward run-ins on the beach, having to defend her friend. She honestly might have liked me better as the underdog.

Dawn judged every move I made. Joe and I were in Las Vegas for work and decided to elope. Lexi and our coworker Ralph were our witnesses at the Little White Wedding Chapel. Somehow Dawn surmised from photos on social media of me in a white dress in Las Vegas that we might have gotten married. Instead of asking me, like an adult, she looked it up in the Clark County, Nevada, marriage records. She then called our mutual friend Polly to create a shitstorm, saying what a horrible person I was for not telling anyone that I spur-of-the-moment eloped. Poor Polly called me crying to ask, "Why didn't you tell me you got married?" I was dumbfounded that it had already spread to Oklahoma. I explained to her that I hadn't even told my son or my mother yet. If this wasn't a scumbag move on Dawn's part, don't ask me what would have been.

So much so that I had to write to Dawn explaining to her that if she told anyone, namely my kids, then we were going to have a *big* problem. She wrote back and told me to never speak to her again, that *I* was toxic. You don't have to ask me twice—done. Right before Cooper left for his freshman year in college, I shared the news with him. In typical Josephs fashion he was thrilled for us, mainly because we didn't spend a fortune on the wedding. More for him.

Over the years, people *can* grow and change. I mourned the loss of my friendship with Dawn for many years, but now we are in a much better place. So much has changed since 2013 that a lot of it is water under the bridge. I'm not a grudge holder. Dawn remains close with all my children, and especially with my daughter. I can't help but feel she's usurped my position in her life, but at least I know that my daughter has a loving female figure by her side.

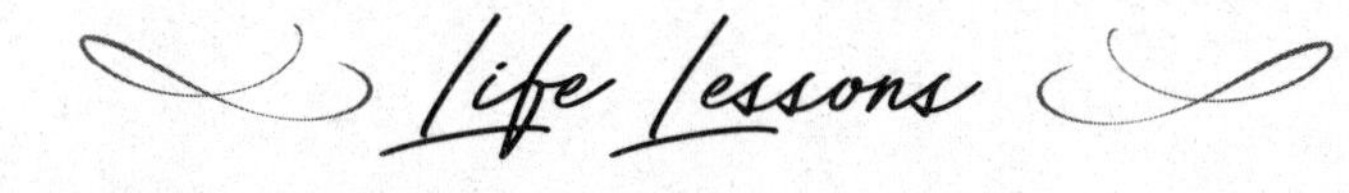

- No one leaves a happy marriage. *Fact.*
- Not everything lasts forever. People change and grow apart, and that's okay.

Chapter Twelve

RENOVATING THE DREAM

Sometimes a "fairy tale" needs a different ending, and this heroine was determined to rewrite her happily ever after. Even though my marriage had unraveled, I decided to create a revised story where all of the same characters remained, just in new roles. In order to do that, it was time to figure out how to extract myself from my old life and move on with my new one.

At this point, everyone knew about me and Jan and about me and Joe—and, remarkably, we were all still alive to talk about it. Remember when Jan was supposed to be house hunting while I was at the beach house? *Yeah, never happened.* He never planned on moving. One of us had to go, so I decided it would just be easier for Joe and me to look for a home nearby to live in with Cooper. This way he could go back and forth between the two of us easily.

It was easier to move because, as I've mentioned, my name was never on the deed for the house, because Jan refused to add it once we were married. I also don't think that Jan would have been able to pull it together to move out. He was still reeling from the fallout. So, after nearly twenty years of marriage, I took the five pieces of furniture that I wanted and my only investment—my wardrobe—and drove the few blocks to my new house. We had found a beautiful ten-bedroom home to rent, with a pool and a theater. We knew it was meant to be, because the owner of the home had grown up in the house that Joe had lived in with his former wife. Not sure why we needed ten bedrooms, but I always did love a sleepover.

We moved two weeks before Christmas, and I felt especially emotional about how the next year was going to be so different. At times like those it was easy to think of the happy memories and push the bad ones to the side, but I knew that my decision was the right one. Everybody has a right to be happy. Jan deserved to be with someone he was madly in love with, and who was madly in love with him, and I deserved the same. I don't think he realized how miserable we were together. I simply couldn't expose Cooper to any more of the bickering, fighting, underlying anxiety, and unspoken resentment. He was the one who was around the most for it, since the other kids were no longer living at home. He deserved to see a happy, healthy relationship. Knowing that I could now give him this was the reassurance that got me through any of my momentary doubts.

It was a relief to be able to operate Macbeth without the worry of having to prove myself to someone else. I didn't have to worry about my work life affecting my home life any longer. Joe and I are in separate businesses, and while we are a team, we respect each other's autonomy in business. This was a welcome change of pace.

One of the few photos I have with my father before we flew the coop.

Sex kitten and her sidekick.

Hide your husbands . . .
Marge Sr. in all her glory.

Farmer Marge at her dance recital . . . pigtails and all.

Every Blondie needs their Brownie (from left: Dolores, me, Jackie, and Jennifer).

The most overpriced pooch in town, Queenie.

Wayne—the only dad I ever knew.

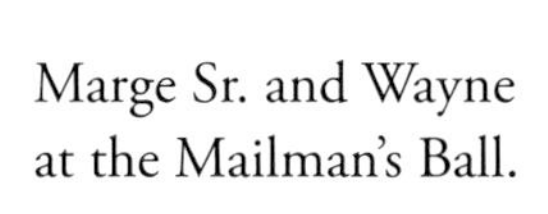

Marge Sr. and Wayne at the Mailman's Ball.

Me and my partner in crime, Stubs.

My Budapest fling.

Rhinestone Cowgirls (from left: Polly, me, and Teresa).

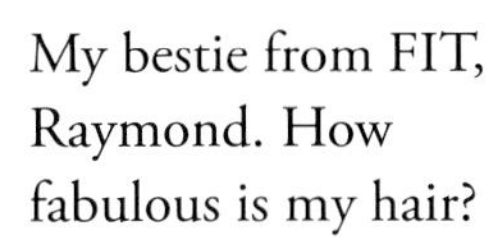

My bestie from FIT, Raymond. How fabulous is my hair?

Two women who have lifted me up from the beginning: my mentor, Vicki (left), and my friend Judy (right).

Who said pigtail extensions were a good idea? *(Photograph by Priscilla DiStasio)*

Officially Mrs. Josephs.

My agent Amy Rosenblum, who helped me get started in the TV world (from left: Amy, me, Chris Burch, and Lexi Barbuto).
(Photograph by Drew Auer)

Honeymooning in Anguilla.

At my Hospital Heroes event with Summer from Brave Gowns and Lexi to my right, and the most amazing kids I have ever been lucky enough to meet.

If it was good enough for Bianca Jagger . . . At my "Studio 50" fiftieth birthday party. *(Photograph by Bret Josephs)*

One of my first headshots. *(Courtesy of the author)*

Boobs and buckets (from left: Jennine Cabrera, me, and Lexi).

The list everyone wants to be on: Oprah's O List. *(Courtesy of the author)*

Team Macbeth (from left: Jennine, Marge Sr., me, Jodi Goldberg, and Lexi).

I pack light.

I told you I'd get these pigtails on *Today*.

Red, white, and cute.

Joe and me with Joan at a party in her apartment—an ICONIC night! *(Photograph by Amy Rosenblum)*

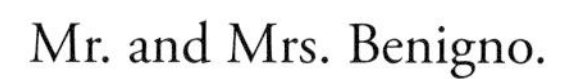

Mr. and Mrs. Benigno.

A little white wedding at A Little White Wedding Chapel.

Backseat driver.

Disruptors in the clubhouse: me and Michael Rapaport.

My *Watch What Happens Live* debut. *(Photograph by Joe Benigno)*

The right side of the couch (from left: Jackie, Melissa, and me).
(Photograph by Julius Michael)

Daddy and who's your daddy?

Jersey girls can be scary . . .
(from left: Jennifer, Melissa, Jackie, Teresa, me, and Dolores).

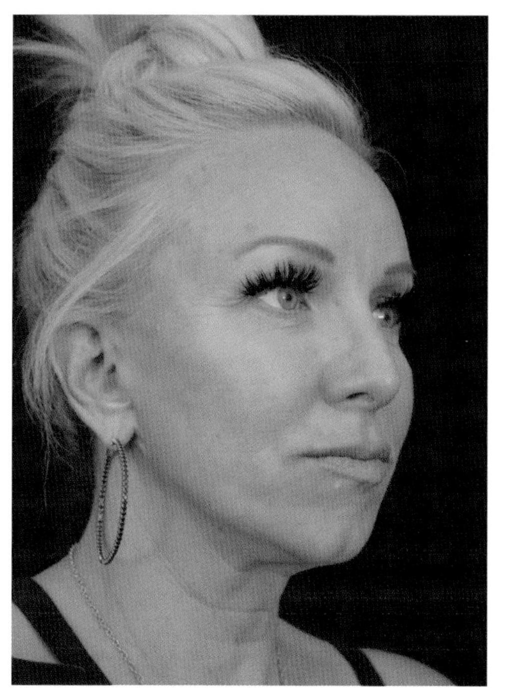

New face, who dis? *(courtesy of Dr. Mark Karolak)*

Seas the day with my Jersey crew (from left: top: Emily Liebert and Lexi; bottom: Jennifer, me, Jackie, Dolores, and Teresa).

Raising the next generation of blonde dreamers—me with Lexi and Nino.

Outside of our world, the whole town was giving their two cents on our relationship. The word on the street was *Oh my God, Margaret left her husband for the contractor*. I guess it was hot gossip. I didn't let it bother me, and certainly Joe didn't give a shit what anyone said or thought about us, but that didn't mean that Cooper wasn't affected by it. He said to me, "You're moving right in with Joe. What do you think that looks like?"

We didn't discuss the infidelity in detail at this time, but I knew Cooper was definitely more than pissed off about it. At the same time, he oddly understood it. I laid it on the line like this: *Things happen in a marriage that you don't plan for. People change. Everyone has flaws and makes mistakes, even your parents.*

The thing I found out about infidelity is that it's judged as the harshest crime you can commit. People are sooner to forgive money laundering or a DWI with children in the car. But when you're unfaithful in your marriage, forget about it. I think that when people catch wind of an infidelity in their town, the first thing they do is look at their own marriage under a microscope. In some people's eyes, once you're labeled a cheater, it will negate every good thing you ever do. You could win a Pulitzer Prize, but you'll still be a cheater who won the Pulitzer Prize.

Thankfully, Jan and I both had so much love for our children that we made sure to have an amicable legal divorce settlement, so as to not drag the kids through more. Basically, I caved to everything. I mean, I gave up my fucking house that I had lived in for twenty years. Even though my name wasn't on the paperwork, I was still entitled to a certain percentage of the home and everything in it, but

I didn't put up a fight. I asked for nothing. I expected nothing. I just handed Jan whatever he wanted, which included alimony.

Can you believe that? He actually asked for spousal support because I was doing so well financially, and I was just like, *Fine, I'll give it to him.* I didn't consider myself for the future. I didn't expect any speed bumps, which was a mistake. I was hit with lawsuits, and I foolishly hadn't planned for anything like that. This is one place where my optimism bit me in the ass. The problem was that I was always concerned about everybody else and how my actions were going to impact my family. I didn't want to do anything that would upset them. I harbored some guilt, and I wanted to give Jan what he asked for without a fight. I felt sorry for him, which was a mistake. While I worried about everyone else, no one was looking out for me.

Jan never went back to work. He lives a much simpler life than I do and he's very happy. He would say that I live a chaotic life, but I'm very happy. I support a lot of people. I have a business, I have a staff, and I'm always working toward the next goal.

I had always thrown fabulous holiday parties, and this year was going to be bigger and better than ever. I thought to myself, *If everyone in our town is going to talk, they're going to talk right to my face. I'm going to put all my business out there.* I knew that once everyone saw how happy Joe and I were, the gossip would be yesterday's news in a hot minute. How could they talk shit while stuffing their faces with my pigs in a blanket? I invited a hundred of my closest friends and business associates to the enormous holiday housewarming bash. It was a beautiful catered affair on Christmas Day. Since most of my friends were Jewish, it worked out perfectly . . . They didn't have to eat Chinese food.

It was also a deep sigh of relief and an aha moment because everything just felt so right. Marge Sr. slept over; we all opened gifts together in the morning and shared a beautiful family breakfast with Cooper and Joe's children. I felt at home and like we could move our lives forward. It was easy, unlike years past. This is no insult to Jan, but when we threw our parties, there would inevitably be a day of crying beforehand. Jan always loved our parties, but only after the fact. He would say the next morning, *Sweetie, that was a terrific night.* This was the first year that I didn't cry on Christmas. It was weird to feel that something was wrong because it went off without any hitches. I was always waiting for the other shoe to drop.

Cooper was adjusting to our new normal very well. Unfortunately, his brother Dean and sister, Tori, had been upset with me since the summer, and things weren't looking up. They were barely talking to me because they disapproved of my relationship with Joe, not to mention us moving in together so fast. My oldest son, Bret, was fine with it, on the other hand. He has a hard relationship with his father, which is another story in and of itself. Not a day went by when I wasn't hoping that Dean and Tori would come around. I was constantly trying to maintain contact; I would call them, send letters and gifts on holidays, but nothing much changed. I even fully furnished Tori's New York City apartment and paid part of the rent on it.

The reality that some of my children became collateral damage was very hard for me. They didn't understand that my marriage to Jan was hopeless and that I couldn't remain the best version of myself by staying where I was. Everybody was drowning. If I didn't save myself, I couldn't save anyone. For that reason and many others, I knew I'd made the right decision, even though it was deeply painful. It really made life better for everybody, including my ex-husband, who's much happier now.

Everything that I did was in the best interests of my children, even if they couldn't see it at the time. They are my entire life. I spent nearly every waking moment with them for two decades, talking to them every day and devoting every thought I had to them. I wouldn't make a move without their best interests at heart, and I definitely did not expect that divorcing their father and moving on with Joe would define me in their eyes. I wasn't stupid—I knew it was going to come with its repercussions. Like I have said before, there were no rash decisions. A tremendous amount of consideration went into it. It took two full years of therapy for Jan and me to conclude that we had to go our separate ways. I knew I was the best and most devoted mother that I could be. I love them all so much. It's never the child's responsibility to make the parent okay. It's always the parents' responsibility to make the child okay, no matter what age they are.

I think they haven't been able to forgive me because when I met them, in my opinion, they felt very abandoned by their own mother, and I swooped in and saved them. And when I ended up leaving Jan, I believe they felt abandoned again. Not only were they hurt but they saw their father hurt. I knew my kids were grown up and had their own lives, and in my head I figured we would continue to spend time together and exist as a newly conceived, unconventional family. I imagined that everything would remain the same with my children and that Jan and I could stay friends. I assumed that we could all progress as different players. *Eternal optimism stings once again.*

One part of my wishful thinking came true. Jan and I have remained friends. He comes over to the house for coffee. We make lunch plans for when Cooper comes into town. Jan and his girlfriend are always invited to our parties. If we see somebody we know in common, we call each other up and gossip on the phone. I still look at him as my family. Sometimes I wonder if he feels as close to me. I think he does, in his own way. Since we've been divorced, I've had tragedies happen. I've taken financial hits and he's been much more liquid than I've been, so he's generously lent me money and bailed me out of crises. There's no boundary with us. I never felt like I was losing my best friend, because we're better friends now than we were when we were married. We both don't have to put up with each other's nonsense. As he often says, *You don't have to hide your packages in the trunk anymore.* It's funny that I'm much more comfortable telling him certain things now than I was when we were together. Joe is very secure in himself, so he never feels threatened by my new normal with Jan; he understands that we will always be in each other's lives.

Amazingly, Jan and Joe even get along now. Do they love each other? Not so much. Jan still thinks Joe stole his wife. But I don't think he really wanted this wife. I don't think he'd be happy in this life. I'm too much of a whirlwind. I could stress anybody out. I mean, let's be honest, I make coffee nervous. I'm 100 percent at all times, and sometimes 150 percent. I'm a ball of energy—constantly running, thinking, and doing. My mind doesn't stop spinning. I can achieve in a day what most people can achieve in a month. And that's the opposite of how Jan is. The good thing is, we know that now and can coexist peacefully.

It's heart-wrenching that some of my kids are not part of that, but at least all my children are close with one another, which is extremely important to me. Just knowing that they're doing well and are content in their lives provides me solace. As long as they're succeeding and have healthy relationships, how can I complain? Jan tells me that he tries to convince them to forgive me, and I have total faith in that, because he knows that I'm suffering.

Probably the biggest blow was not being invited to Dean's wedding a number of years ago. I didn't get out of bed for a week. It stung me to know that my former best friend Dawn was there. Even Eviline, his birth mother, got an invite, and she never even made it to his college graduation. Cooper called me from California, where it took place, crying that I wasn't included. My memory was erased from the whole event; I was actually even cut out of family photos, like I'd never existed. If I had been invited, even the day before, I would have gotten on the red-eye in two seconds. Needless to say, it was a very rough time for me. To this day, it still is.

Jan wanted Dean to extend an olive branch, but it didn't happen. Jan sent me pictures the day of. It was very bittersweet. I wanted so badly to be there, but I was also so relieved to know that he'd found the love of his life. I sent him a text the morning of the wedding wishing him and his bride all the happiness in the world.

She's the most amazing wife I could have wished for my son, and I'm so grateful to know that her family has embraced him as one of their own.

Dean has two beautiful children now, whom I hope to meet one day. I get to see pictures of them via social media and when Cooper visits. I text Dean long messages and thankfully he responds. Albeit with very short answers, but beggars can't be choosers. I send gifts for birthdays and holidays. I'd love nothing more than to be a part of their lives. It's very surreal that Dean and I were so close and now we're not. The space between us has caused my memories with him to almost feel like a beautiful dream. The last time that we were physically together was at my mother-in-law's funeral in December 2017. As devastated as I was to lose my mother-in-law, I felt so lucky to be in the same room as my children again. Even to hug and kiss them that one day gave me so much hope for our future.

My relationship with Tori is even more strained, if you can believe that. She carries a lot of resentment toward me. Her text messages to me aren't filled with any sweetness. She was only a little girl, eight years old, when I showed up. She was my everything. She would sleep in my bed and was Cooper's second mommy. Now she is married and has a beautiful little girl of her own. I know she's the best mommy because that is what she was born to do.

I cling to the fact that everybody ended up happy in the end. I will forever be distraught that I can't be with all of my children. Yet, nine years later, I still hold out hope and pray that something will change. I would love nothing more than that. I will always be here for them if they ever want to pick up the phone. I would drop everything.

- Every choice has a consequence.
- Life is bittersweet. Sometimes you will mourn parts of your life while embarking on new chapters.
- It is never the child's responsibility to make the parent okay. It is always the parent's responsibility to comfort the child, no matter the age.

Chapter Thirteen

BRINGING IN THE BIG GUNS

Now it's time to talk about how my business really started to take off. Back when Jan and I were still together and I was on the trade show circuit, all the larger stores wanted to know what I could sell to them. Our style was the perfect mix of preppy bohemian: acid-bright colors, swirling prints and patterns. This always caught the eye of the larger retailers, like Bed Bath & Beyond and HomeGoods. They started asking me, *Margaret, what can we buy from you?* I said, *Nothing, I'm made in America. I'm too expensive.* I was a snobby bitch and somewhat naïve. I loved selling to places like Neiman Marcus and the smaller specialty boutiques. It wasn't until Jonathan Breiter, a prominent licensing agent in the industry, walked into the booth and said, "You really should start licensing out your brand; you have a great look and everyone wants you," that I started to change. He explained that, basically, it would be my style and my brand, and then I could branch out to all different products, because various manufacturers would take my brand and put my look onto their products so they could distribute them to the larger mass retailers at a high volume and a low margin. This concept was totally foreign to me. If it's foreign for you too, let me explain. High volume = massive quantity. Low margin = less profit. Massive quantity + less profit = a lot of money. My volume wasn't high, but my margins were huge. I had full control of my product because I had my own factory, but in truth I was having trouble producing a sufficient amount of inventory for the shops I was already in. Then I'd get something called a royalty, which was essentially a percentage of those sales, since everything would have my name, style, and logo attached to it. He told me to put together a brand deck and that they'd start farming me out. I said, "That sounds amazing, but it almost sounds too good to be true." Like I said before, you have to make for the masses to eat with the classes.

This was a pivotal moment for me, both personally and professionally. At this point, as my business was on the incline, my marriage was on a steep decline. Things weren't good, and I kept thinking, *How am I going to change my business to stay afloat if Jan and I split up?* This was a major big-girl-panties moment for me.

So Lexi, Jennine, and I, the triple threat, started designing a brand deck with all the press we'd done, including information about the business, our prints and patterns, and the powerhouse in pigtails that sat at the helm, aka *moi* (said in the voice of Ms. Piggy). By the way, we'd never designed a brand deck before and had no fucking clue what we were doing, had never even seen one. Needless to say, we nailed it. Lucky for us, there was no one who looked like us in the market in 2009. We were totally unique, refreshing, and had a point of view.

Naturally, Jonathan thought the deck was great too. He immediately started shopping us around to get us some deals. Right out of the gate, not even two weeks later, he had meetings set up. One of them was with a company called Parker Concepts that manufactures home storage, kitchen accessories, etc. I'll never forget walking into that showroom. I was in my early forties—blonde, tan, and youthful, with my boobs on display. Needless to say, I was as foreign a concept to them as they were to me. They looked me up and down, took it all in, and then told me how much they loved my prints and patterns. They were selling me on just how much they could grow my brand with their product. They thought we'd be a great fit and wanted to see all my designs on their aprons, pot holders, ironing board covers, and closet storage. Two days later I received my first contract, with a $15K advance and a 5 percent royalty, to sign on the spot.

I did the math, and 5 percent of a few million dollars a year in addition to money up front sounded like a cakewalk to me. In comparison to running my own factory and dealing with screaming Bar Mitzvah mothers who didn't get their centerpieces in time, this was just what I needed. I didn't have to make anything. I just had to help design it and then collect my percentage. I was thinking, *What's wrong with this deal?* Nothing. So I was like, *A table for four at Buddakan, extra lobster fried rice please.*

Little did I know . . . there was a lot more to come. When something seems too good to be true, it usually is. Meanwhile, I thought Parker Concepts was fabulous and worked particularly closely with their in-house licensing director, Ralph. In fact, I'm still in business with him today, despite the fact that he's since left the company. (That's a story for down the road.) So we started working with Parker Concepts, and it took off like a house on fire. Everybody loved our look. Parker had meetings with buyers from every major retailer, and the orders just started flowing in. All the buyers knew Macbeth from the years of trade shows and were thrilled to finally be able to access the brand.

The Parker product line was the talk of the industry, and my brand was becoming very established in this new space. Macbeth Collection put the fun into functionality. Believe it or not, no one had ever thought to put a pink paisley on a step stool. Though now it's commonplace, Macbeth truly was the first. We were known to be pioneers of twinning prints. Unexpected combinations were definitely a signature of mine and made Macbeth stand out from the crowd. It was a high-end look that brought fashion into everyday utilitarian items. Let's face it, I made a tin bucket into the hottest item in the Hamptons. Revolutionizing the mass market space was the natural next step. Parker Concepts couldn't believe how quickly it took off, and they were calling all their friends about me. I had no idea that the licensing industry was basically run by one community, and everybody was a brother, cousin, uncle, or related by marriage. Initially, this worked out great for me. Nothing is better than a recommendation from a dear friend or family member. Shortly thereafter I was connected with a tech accessory company, Neptune International, which I knew nothing about. But he was best friends with one of the Parker boys, so I thought, *Let me give it a whirl.*

I told Lexi I was going downtown with my licensing agent to see what Neptune had to offer. Obviously, I was not thinking clearly, because as soon as I'd been introduced to these men, I called Lexi and Jennine and said, "Oh my God, they're so good-looking; we have to sign the deal." I still knew very little about the licensing business, but I sure knew hot guys. I was like, *How bad could it be to work with these cuties? They're writing me a check and they're going to pay me a 6 percent royalty.* That was up a percentage from the other guys, which makes a big difference when you're talking millions. I knew nothing about iPhone cases or headphones, but I did know about color, prints, patterns, design, and what a girl wants. Before you knew it, we were the first printed tech accessory brand in Walmart. Business just started rolling in. Prior to this, tech accessories were strictly *boooorrring*. This was an untapped market. Put it this way: When we showed up at CES (a trade show organized by the Consumer Technology Association), we were the box of crayons in a strictly black and gray world. Neptune might have brought us to the table, but we changed the game.

I was just so thrilled that we were making money and growing rapidly. Parker Concepts, my original licensee, saw the growth potential for my brand and they wanted in. They offered to buy out my soon-to-be-ex-husband and take a partnership stake. Of course, I didn't tell them he was my soon-to-be-ex-husband. I was like, *Let them buy him out.* Truthfully, this came as a blessing, because it allowed Jan peace of mind and me a clear path to separate my personal and business lives. I knew he would be calmer not having to deal with the ups and downs of our business. My career was about to explode, my brand was in almost every store I walked into, and this was just the beginning. Jan was approaching retirement, and the only thing he was ready for was a round of golf. In Parker, I thought, I'd have a phenomenal business partner who knows how to run a domestic production and understands global licensing. I would be the front person and handle the design, the styling, and the marketing—everything I excelled in and that came so naturally to me—and they'd bring to the table their expertise in distribution, importing, and licensing. They also had the capital to grow my brand beyond my capability.

It was clear to both Jan and me that our marriage was over. We were getting separated, so we cut the deal, which left Jan with a generous buyout. It also meant that I would keep my 50 percent of the company and Parker Concepts would get their 50 percent. It all seemed wonderful. At first.

A couple of changes immediately came into play. Parker Concepts arranged for our employees to move to their warehouse an hour away. Additionally, they changed the way we did our production. Our employees were paid on a bonus scale, by the piece. Which in essence came to way above minimum wage. It worked out to about $25 an hour. Parker Concepts thought that this was a gross overpayment. So they shifted the pay structure to an hourly wage, and almost overnight our production shifted from a samba to a slow waltz. The incentive for our team to produce and take home a great paycheck was immediately gone. So was our ability to deliver on the huge number of orders we were receiving daily.

I was like, *I don't think that's the best idea.* But they assured me that they knew how to run a business, and I believed them. After all, they had a half-million-square-foot warehouse, a team of over one hundred people, and close to a hundred-million-dollar business. Who was I to question them? They wanted to manage and control everything, and that was what I wanted too. I didn't want to have to handle all of it by myself, even if it meant growing pains.

Then something else happened that I wasn't comfortable with. I realized that Parker Concepts hadn't put my name on the bank account. They couldn't understand why it was so important to me to have my name on the bank account. *Why do you care if your name's not on it? Whenever you want money, just ask us.* I was having flashbacks to Jan's crazy financial tyranny . . . *Did I just trade one husband for another?* Again, I was in this awkward position where I was thinking, *Okay, I'm going to be making a lot of dough. Should I just let this go?* I was already getting 55 percent of the profits, which was a bigger percentage than they were getting. And they said, *We'll handle it. We have a controller. He'll cut the checks when you need them.* It definitely seemed like the path of least resistance; however, it also made me feel like I was an employee of my own company, instead of the founder and partner that I was. Naturally, if something was equitably mine—my idea, my concept, my designs, my brand—I didn't know why I would have to ask. But, somehow, here I was, asking for the checks to be cut.

Right from the beginning I should have been strong enough to say, *No, my name needs to be on the bank account.* But of course, it was presented to me as if it wasn't a big deal. And, to be honest, I was too nervous to speak up, for fear of jeopardizing my fiscal security. I was getting divorced from Jan and I was on the hook for a large amount of alimony. I was growing my business, making a lot more money than I was used to, and licenses were coming in. There was so much on the line that I acquiesced to things I shouldn't have acquiesced to at the outset, like the fact that now my employees had to go much farther to the factory, to make less money. It didn't sit well with me. I told Parker Concepts that if they changed the pay structure of the staff, their productivity was going to decrease, and that would hurt my domestic business, which it did. That was very upsetting. All of a sudden I was in a place where my licensing was doing great and my made-to-order luxury business wasn't, so that was an issue. I asked them to go back to the old way of doing things, but they said no, and I felt like there was nothing I could do about it. My hands were tied. The most upsetting thing was that Parker Concepts couldn't understand that the success of my high-end domestic business had driven the success of my licensing business. Put it this way: Without a Fifth Avenue flagship, Calvin Klein wasn't selling hundreds of millions of pairs of underpants in TJ Maxx, and the same went for me. That's the nature of the beast.

I should have spoken up immediately. That's on me. Only whenever I did say something, they always claimed I was being unreasonable and dramatic. I do think that I was treated completely differently for being a woman in a company run by men; it was apparent and glaringly discriminatory. They would say to me, *Why are you so hysterical? We've been in business a long time; we know better.* I was being treated like a ditz. This was coming from people who didn't even know who Mick Jagger and Beyoncé were. The same people who thought that Hurricane Sandy was a repercussion of gay marriage being legalized in New York. Need I say more?

If I said something to the controller, they would tell me, *He doesn't work with women, it's a religious thing*. I was like, *What religion is that?* We all know this is absolute bullshit. Who would hire someone like that to work with women all day, then? Parker Concepts and Macbeth Collection were both filled with female employees.

The controller also wanted to set a dress code for women in the company, because he didn't like the way the girls wore their skirts. Guess what? I didn't like the crumbs in his beard, but I didn't say anything. It seemed even more ridiculous, considering that he crept around drooling over girls' ankles at every given moment. Everybody was dressed very tastefully, and it was just one too many opinions from someone who didn't own the company . . . Needless to say, his dress code was never approved. If anyone was authorized to set a dress code, it was me. And you can be sure I wouldn't have outlawed skirts. In my honest opinion, I don't think religion should have an impact in the workplace. I cannot enforce my beliefs on my employees.

Do I wish I'd been more assertive? *Yes, I do*. I've learned from my mistakes, though. My advice to other women who find themselves in similar situations is that you have to be confident in your judgment right from the start. Don't be afraid to stand up for yourself and what's right. If it doesn't sit well with you, say it, lay it on the line, and make sure that it's *your* name on your bank account and your company. Don't let someone control you just because *they appear* smarter than you or have been in business longer than you; it doesn't make a difference. You don't need to ask for permission to take your own money. That's what happened to me, even though I had a fair contract that was written by an attorney. In my opinion, the men I worked with felt like our contract was open to interpretation, and I didn't want to rock the boat and say, *This isn't what the contract says.* I didn't want to be adversarial, because I wanted the deal to work. Ironically, this doomed the deal from the start. I was left feeling overpowered in my own company and resentful. On the other hand, *they* felt resentful that I made so much money as a woman who had a husband at home, and don't think they didn't say this to me. *Why do you need to make so much? You have a husband.*

The thing is, it's *better* to rock the boat sometimes. Business is business. If you start off on the wrong foot and let people take advantage of you, that means you're not setting boundaries properly and the boundaries will always be pushed. You have to define things very clearly from day one; otherwise there's a real risk that everything will fall apart, despite your best intentions. You are the only person who has your best interests truly at heart. Trust your gut, stand up for yourself, and don't put up with any shit.

Occupational drama aside, at this point I was living with Joe and things were truly amazing between us. We were very happy, and our life was going just the way that I had hoped—fabulously. It was a nice change of pace to be able to go to Joe for advice without feeling like his guidance was tainted the way it had been with Jan. Often I would run something by Joe and he'd say, *This doesn't feel right. I wouldn't be comfortable with that.* I trust him implicitly and value his advice and opinion.

I would also bounce things off Lexi. I was never blind to the fact that my judgment could be wrong. I was dealing with men who were very dismissive, who weren't used to working with women, and who didn't understand boundaries. It was a game I wasn't ready to play, so there were plenty of times when I questioned myself. It always seemed like I was on the back foot. Sure, it was great that we were making so much money, but that success came with a price. I never felt in control of my own company or my own decisions, which is unacceptable. I know that now.

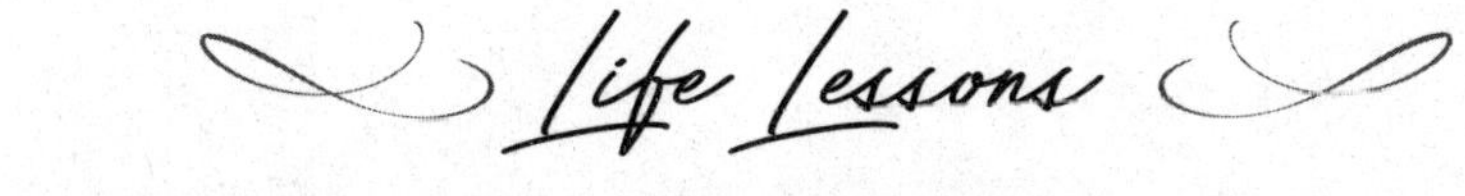

- Don't take yourself out of the game before you know how to play it or what the prize is.
- Just because someone's called a partner doesn't mean you share the same vision.
- Don't be afraid to speak up because someone appears more experienced than you on paper.

Chapter Fourteen

MARGE IN CHARGE

It was 2012, and I really felt like I had hit the jackpot. My business was booming, and I was finally reaping the rewards of all my hard work. Joe and I were living together in a beautiful home. Cooper was with us. We were traveling all over the place—to Europe, St. Barts, renting beach houses, you name it. I had amassed eleven licensees, who were all thriving. We were selling to every major retailer and raking in tens of millions of dollars at Walmart, and that was just in tech accessories. Basically, we were killing it on every front.

Despite my issues with Parker concerning my domestic production, everything was still running successfully, if not as fast or as smoothly as I wanted it to. I had a huge creative team that worked out of the first floor of our house. They were developing so many new concepts that we couldn't get them on the shelves quick enough. In addition, our domestic production was still moving along, although not as fast as I would have liked. I was flying to trade shows all over the country and garnering a lot of publicity along the way.

Our brand recognition was fabulous; you could find us in almost any style and design magazine on the rack. You couldn't miss our signature prints and patterns in eye-popping color—they grabbed you, demanding your attention. Macbeth was loved internationally, from the UK to Canada to Japan. If there was a hot store, you could be sure they carried their fair share of Macbeth buckets. I truly couldn't believe that I'd grown my little company from my kitchen table into a global lifestyle brand. My products were even in Oprah's and Jennifer Aniston's kitchens. Not to name-drop . . . but we were a celebrity fave. As much as I had to pinch myself that I had done this, I also had to pat myself on the back because this had been *no* easy ride.

Since I had achieved all this success, CNBC was interested in doing a segment on me called "Moms Making Millions." *Listen*, even *I* had to go to media training. I'd never been on television before. So I went to meet with these women, Amy Rosenblum, who was a media coach and former senior producer at the *Today* show, and Jane Hanson, who was a well-known TV anchor and host. I showed up with my pigtails in and my boobs out, the normal Marge style. Amy immediately challenged me and my pigtails: "Oh my God, you can't come on CNBC with those pigtails. Who's going to take you seriously like that?" Of course, I wasn't having that and replied, "What the hell are you talking about? I'm not taking out my fucking pigtails. What kind of craziness is that?" She was like, "Okay, I see. You're a real character, aren't you?" I thought about it for a split second and said, "I guess I am." Honestly, I'd never thought of myself in that way, but if it got me on TV, I was fine with it.

I prepped with Amy and Jane, and of course showed up ready to put on a show at CNBC. Pigtails and all. The funny thing about being on a segment called "Moms Making Millions" is that everyone is automatically like, *Oh, you're a multimillionaire*. But the truth is that while we were doing $60 to $70 million in retail, that was not all going in my bank account. In other words, when people say that a company is doing $100 million, for example, it does not mean that they're actually taking home that much money. They profit a fraction of that after overhead, production costs, and employees are paid. That's where things get misconstrued and perceptions are false. Put it this way, I was making everybody else millions. Regardless, I was thrilled to be picked for the show.

I got a taste of the on-air experience and knew that this was an area in which I wanted to expand my career. Amy and I immediately fell in love and started working together. After my success on CNBC, Amy started booking me on all the morning shows as a lifestyle expert, doing segments such as "Marge's Holiday Gift Ideas," "Marge's Father's Day Picks," and "Marge Throws a Party on a Budget." It was second nature to me, and I could make any event look super-expensive on a dime, which viewers were very interested in. You, as readers, are also probably interested, so let me give you a few ideas. For example, on the Fourth of July we spray-painted three pineapples red, white, and blue to stand as the centerpiece. This took all of five minutes and a trip to the grocery store, but people were talking about the creative centerpieces all night. If you don't have a serving tray, you can just grab a cute clipboard (maybe your Macbeth Collection one) to use as a makeshift platter, tucking the cocktail napkins under the clip. If you don't have the most expensive champagne or wine at your bar, you can dip-dye the bottles in colored glitter to glam them up. There's always a way to elevate your event on a budget.

Lexi and I were amazing at endlessly pulling rabbits out of a hat, and we were showing everybody else how to do it too. The cherry on top was that every segment was also an opportunity to market my own products and include a piece from my own collection. A free ad, presented by the person who designed the product. What better way to grow the reach for my personal brand as well as Macbeth?

Now, when I say *all* the morning shows, I mean *almost* all the morning shows. The *Today* show, an NBC property, did not want The Marge and her pigtails in all their glory in the 9 a.m. hour. They figured I'd be too much for their viewers to handle before their second cup of coffee. Ironically, Bravo, an NBC property, is now my home. Although I did eventually make it on the *Today* show with a Father's Day gifting guide, and made sure to wear my pigtails. All thanks to Amy.

My funny, quirky, fast-on-my-feet demeanor was perfect for prime time. No matter the task, I could always deliver. Amy knew I was the real deal and came to me, saying, "You need your own reality show; I'm pitching you to production companies. But before I do that . . . you need your eyes done, honey, and maybe a little Botox." Anyone else would have cried, left, or punched her. I was like, *No problem. Consider it done.* It takes a certain breed to succeed in the harsh world of television, and I was a thoroughbred. I wasn't prepared to ditch my pigtails or hide my boobs, but I galloped right to the plastic surgeon. Now, Amy might sound like a bitch, but she was right and she wanted to present the best version of me she could.

It was my first foray into plastic surgery and it was not a big deal at all. I went to Thomas Romo in New York City. I'll never forget that I said to him, "I need to have my lids done. I'm wrinkly." As I've said before, I'm a professional know-it-all and an amateur doctor. He took one look at me and said, "Babe, I'm the doctor. I'll tell you what you need. You need to lift the curtain rod before you hem the curtains; hence, you need a brow lift." Turns out he was right. I booked my appointment into Lenox Hill and got my brow lift and lids done for a *mere* $17,000. Which for some reason felt like a bargain at the time. *I obviously had no fucking clue.*

Of course, Amy had to film the whole thing and add it to my sizzle reel so she could shop me around, which she did. Very quickly, three big production companies were interested: Magilla Entertainment, Vidiots, and Left Right. Magilla Entertainment was best known for *Long Island Medium* and *Duck Dynasty*. For various reasons, we opted to go with them, and I was very excited about what the future had in store.

The show they were looking to create was tentatively titled *Marge in Charge*, and it was the perfect mix of creativity and chaos. We were meant for it because *everything* was always crazy in our home. We had a full cast of characters working there every day—including my mother—who'd been part of growing the brand from scratch. Joe was also in and out, even though he had his own business of crazy characters who loved to stop by for coffee and crumb cake to break up the day. It was insane. We couldn't change who we were if we tried. Not that we wanted to. Sure, we were a little unprofessional, but that was the special sauce.

There'd be important documents all over the kitchen table while I was cooking everyone waffles in my pajamas, braless, wearing a weave. A look that I've committed to on many occasions—in fact, I'm wearing it as I write this. Why I was cooking the waffles is beyond me; I had Lidia, our cook, living with us too. But we all know, as this chapter (and the series at the time) is titled, The Marge likes to be in charge. Anyway, we were doing major business deals, moving and shaking in the right direction, and at the same time, my mother was fucking up the books on a regular basis. The woman never paid my bills punctually. Though she'd worked for plenty of other people and paid *their* bills promptly, for some reason she couldn't do the same for me. She was always getting a manicure or having her hair done and saying, *Sweetie, you know I have to look good. You don't want me to look like shit*—as my cellphone was getting shut off.

I was screaming at her incessantly, even though she seemed busy. She always appeared to be on the computer or shipping UPS boxes, but I'm not exactly sure what she was doing. She would answer the phone and never even bother to screen my calls. I mean, someone could have asked to murder me and she would have said, *She's upstairs in the bedroom, in the closet; you can go find her.* She was TMI Marge Sr. as per usual and would give out my phone number to anybody who inquired. It was completely ridiculous; I'm surprised she didn't write it on the bathroom wall. We thought for sure we were going to get the reality show. How could we not?!

Amy had simultaneously launched her new company, Media Masters, as I was being prepped for CNBC. To celebrate the early success, her close friend Joan Rivers threw her a party in her Manhattan apartment. I was one of Amy's most promising clients, and she was convinced that I was headed for big things in the TV space. Amy was so excited to introduce me to Joan, and I was intimidated and elated at the same time. I was so grateful that Joe was beside me to hold my hand and share in the moment. I don't know who loved Joan more, me or Joe. Her apartment made you feel like you were in an Italian opera house and the Palace of Versailles all at the same time. It had balconies, gold-leaf accents—it was from another era. I can't even do it justice—just google it. Joan was larger than life but also so tiny. I towered over her like I had just birthed her in my stripper heels. For someone known for her wisecracks and cutting comments on the carpet, in person she was attentive, sweet, and humble. You could even say she was a bit shy. Joe and I cuddled up next to her for a photo and I said, "Joe, don't grab Joan's ass!" She quickly came back with "What are you talking about? That's what I was hoping for—he's so cute." Joe then squeezed her and kissed her cheek. That night she said to me and Joe, "You two are real class acts. You're the only people who brought me a gift. I mean, what's with all these other people? No manners." Legit, who in their right mind walks into an event at Joan Rivers's home and doesn't bring something for the hostess? Not The Marge. I guess no one there had watched my hostess gift segment on CBS. I gave her a beautifully ornate Edgar Berebi picture frame embellished with crystals from Bergdorf Goodman, which she loved. What she loved even more was the gift wrapping because it had a big gold metal tassel with burgundy silk fringe attached. She immediately put the tassel on her necklace and wore it around the party all night. That was classic.

Later that evening, in one of the most memorable moments of my life, Joan took me aside and said, "Listen, you're very smart. You don't look like everybody else. Those pigtails make you stand out. Don't ever change that." I told her how many people had encouraged me to change, and she admitted that the same thing had happened to her when she was first starting out, but that she stuck to who she was. She said, "It took me a longer time to be successful because of that, and I was down for a while, but it was worth it. It makes a difference to stand out. You don't want to fit in. That's what separates you from everyone else." I thanked her profusely for her advice. I was so grateful just to have been in her presence. That year she sent me a Christmas ornament. I was thrilled to have made the list. There will never be anybody like her. Joan, *you* were the ultimate class act.

Marge in Charge did not get picked up immediately, which came as a surprise to everyone involved. There were many networks interested, but we couldn't seem to land anywhere solid. It was 2013 and I was still under contract when, out of the blue, the *Real Housewives of New Jersey* casting team approached me. The casting director had seen my lifestyle TV segments and thought I would be a great fit. I thought, *What do I have to lose?* So I filmed a tape and naturally they picked me. Just my luck—I was still tied to the deal with Magilla Entertainment for my own show, so I couldn't accept. I was like, *Okay, the timing isn't right. Forget it. No big deal.*

I definitely didn't regret it. Everyone was saying, *Don't worry, timing is everything*. Obviously, years later that proved to be true, but in the moment, I was still committed to the idea of selling a show that centered around my business. Joe was also totally into the idea of *Marge in Charge*. We both thought it would be fun to share our wild shenanigans with the rest of the world. Even my son Cooper, who has never wanted to be in the spotlight, was willing to tolerate this show. Unfortunately my own show never panned out, and life went on.

I wasn't officially divorced yet, but I was already paying temporary alimony to Jan. I wasn't as worried about taking care of myself as I should have been. I was like, *You know what, if I'm doing well, it's only fair that everybody does well.* I'm still very much of that mentality. I'm all about supporting everybody else, as long as I can. The unfortunate thing is that when everything is flourishing, you never think it's going to reverse itself. But there were some unpleasant times ahead. I just didn't know it yet, and at the moment I was on top of the world.

Skip to 2013: My divorce goes through, and a week later Joe, Lexi, Ralph, and I were on a plane to Las Vegas for a licensing show. Joe told me, "There's no way I went through all this and you're going to pull a stunt and not marry me. We're going to Vegas and we're getting married." We literally planned everything as we were flying there. I wasn't rushing to get married, but I could tell that Joe really wanted to and I was madly in love with him.

I knew I wanted to be with Joe forever. It's just that I'm a less traditional person than he is. I was like, *Why do we have to be married?* But you know, it would be cheaper to be married on the health insurance policy. I also had weird guilt feelings. My divorce was fresh off the press, and I was worried about how my kids were going to feel. But I'd been living with Joe for a year and a half, so the divorce was really just a piece of paper. Everyone had moved on.

It was June 19, 2013, and we booked the Little White Wedding Chapel. I wore a beautiful white Alexis dress, which I'd purchased at Neiman Marcus in Las Vegas. Joe had on a tone-on-tone printed white Etro shirt with white jeans. We got his David Yurman ring there, and I just wore my engagement ring—it was so beautiful. Lexi and Ralph, in head-to-toe pink, were there as our witnesses. We wrote our own vows. Joe's were much more of a tearjerker than mine. When I was writing mine, I was like, *Oh, I'm going to bring this guy to his knees. He's going to be crying.* Little did I know that I'd be in a puddle on the floor from his wildly romantic, heartfelt declaration. But I'll let you be the judge of that . . .

My vows to Joe:

My dearest Joe,

I love and adore you and want you to know my life began when you came into it.

You are the most special man, loving, sweet, affectionate, generous beyond words, kind, super manly, handsome, sexy, beautiful inside and out.

You have made a true home for Cooper and me, and showed us the meaning of love without judgment.

Only you could love and embrace our kookiness with such

tenderness, warmth, and understanding. You have made us better people since having you in our lives and we would be lost without you.

I promise to love, kiss, and take care of you and make you feel like the luckiest man in the world every day. I will forever shower you in cupcakes!

I will make a beautiful home for our little family, Joey, Gina, and Cooper.

I will grow old with you and always see you as my Prince Charming.

I will forever be your pigtail princess.

I love you.

Joe's vows to me:

Margaret,

I love you, with all my heart. You are the best friend I've ever had.

Since we started dating there has never been a doubt in my mind that one day I would marry you, and here we are today.

Over the past four years we have grown inseparable and learned a lot about each other and the pros and cons of wolf packs and I look forward to spending the rest of my life learning a lot more with you.

I love you so much it is hard to put into words.

When I hold you, it is not close enough.

When I kiss you, it is not passionate enough.

Even my most passionate kisses don't come close to show you how much you mean to me.

When we embrace, I know that you feel the same as I do and that is the best feeling in the world.

I am completely happy and never want that feeling to end.

I promise to always be there for you, support you, help you, to always make your life fun and never boring, to give to you all my love, to tell you every day just how beautiful you are.

So I stand here today in front of these two witnesses, Lexi and Ralph, staring into your amazing intense eyes, to ask you the most important question; Will you, Margaret, my best friend, my lover, my soulmate, and my partner-in-crime be my lawful wedded wife?

After the intimate ceremony, we went out to celebrate over sushi at the pan-Asian restaurant Andrea's in the Wynn hotel, where we were staying. It was the perfect end to the day. We managed to make an impromptu wedding become one of the most lasting, loving memories of our lives. The next day we relaxed in a cabana at the topless pool, with our tops on, however. I was Mrs. Benigno now on paper and couldn't be showing my tits to the Las Vegas locals. Plus, it was the middle of the licensing show and we had moved on from Boobs & Buckets. Everyone we knew from the industry was there and we were looking to score more licenses for the brand. As I was working so hard, Joe and I didn't take our honeymoon until a year later. When we did, we did it right. We jaunted to Italy for three and a half weeks to travel through Venice, Florence, Rome, and Capri. We flew first class, which set the tone for the entire trip. We had to buy extra luggage in every city in order to take back everything I was buying along the way. I mean, when we were heading to the airport for our flight home, I made the driver dump his baby seat on the streets of Rome in order to fit the loot. One of my best friends happened to be in Rome for the night. She came to see us off and witnessed the whole incident. She was in an absolute state of panic thinking that we were going to miss our flight. If you've seen the cars in Europe, you know there's not one big enough to handle The Marge.

Now Joe wants to buy a place in Florence, pack his bags, and live there six months of the year. When we're there, everyone calls me Signora Benigno, to his delight. I never changed my last name from Josephs, since my children are Josephs and it's the name associated with my brand. I think sometimes that annoys him. But Margaret Benigno just doesn't roll off the tongue. Listen, I let Joe name the dog after him: Bella Benigno. Who says I'm not romantic?

As I said before, there was no wedding announcement sent out from Vegas. So when we came home, I kept my mouth shut. I didn't tell my mother. I didn't tell Cooper. I didn't tell my friends. I didn't tell anyone. I just wasn't ready. I said, *I'll let them know when the time is right*. That was my prerogative.

Months later, at Thanksgiving, I made the announcement over pumpkin pie. My mother's reaction was typical Marge Sr.: *I wasn't invited. I'm not in the loop. I'm on a need-to-know basis.* Clearly, it was all about her!

When I told Jan, he didn't really react. So I couldn't understand everyone else's hysteria. He's not one to show a ton of emotion. He was like, *Margaret's married, all right, whatever, big deal, da-da-da.* As long as he got his alimony payment, he was content with whatever I did. Joe was also paying alimony to his ex-wife, so a nice big chunk of change was going to our exes monthly.

Thankfully, right now, I'm not paying alimony. Jan graciously took a break from it when my company endured a big lawsuit, which was very nice of him. Like I said previously, I never took any money from the home we shared, and I walked out with five pieces of furniture. I gave up a lot out of guilt. That's on me. I think as women we have to learn that it's okay to take care of ourselves, because if we don't take care of ourselves, we can't take care of anyone else. It's been particularly difficult for me, as my personal and professional lives have been so intertwined. I've made decisions in my life based on emotion instead of sound judgment. It continues to be a challenge, as it is the way I'm wired, but I'm working on it.

At the time, it felt like the right thing to do because my ex-husband was hurt. I did have an affair. I could afford a generous alimony and still live very comfortably. I didn't plan enough for the future—certainly not for a lawsuit or for the fraud that ensued. I figured everything was going to be rosy. Sadly, that's just not the way life is. You have to plan for the future, and you have to ask for what's rightfully yours. Maybe I should have asked for half my house, or at least 25 or 30 percent of it. After all, 30 percent of a million-plus is still a few hundred thousand dollars. I didn't do any of that. Therefore, Jan and I worked out an arrangement, and down the road he bailed me out of a very tough situation. I will be eternally grateful for that.

Fortunately, I have a much better relationship with Jan than Joe has with his ex-wife. She was the last to find out about our marriage. She holds a lot of resentment toward Joe. It wasn't until we were throwing Joe's son a college graduation party that she discovered the news. He'd just finished college and was commissioned by the United States Army as a lieutenant. We'd consulted her about the guest list, and when we sent out the invites it had her name as a host, along with ours, listed as Mr. & Mrs. Joseph Benigno.

She didn't say anything directly to us, but she told their children that she was very taken aback, which was ironic because she was the one to ask Joe for a divorce. They had a different marriage and a different family dynamic than Jan and I did. They led separate lives, whereas Jan and I had a beautiful, amazing family and an extremely close relationship. Moments like this really highlighted how much I had lost, even though I gained so much in my relationship with Joe. I guess she mourned something too. It doesn't matter how much time passes and how many wonderful new memories you create, it's still painful, and a little part of you dies with what you left behind.

Life Lessons

- Be yourself and break the mold instead of conforming to it.
- Missed opportunities aren't missed—they just weren't meant for you at that moment. Timing is everything.
- Don't harbor guilt for taking care of yourself, because if you're not your best self, then you can't be good for anyone else.

Chapter Fifteen

BIG GUNS BACKFIRE

How did I get so lucky to go from being the little girl dipping her Oreos in coffee to having my own global lifestyle brand? It's not luck, it's hard work. *Duh.* But I suffer from *impostor syndrome*. Have you ever heard of it? You might even have it yourself, but never realized that there was a name for it. It's very prevalent in female entrepreneurs and high-achieving individuals. It's defined as a collection of feelings of inadequacy that persists despite evidence of success. It's basically feeling like I'm a kid who snuck over to the grown-ups' table and I'm just waiting to be sent back.

I often catch myself thinking, *Do I deserve this? Am I really this successful? Am I really this smart? Am I going to be found out, because I'm not really who people think I am?* Well, then who the fuck am I? I may have started off "faking it till I make it," but then when I did *make* it, I was left wondering, *Am I fake?*

It's an unfortunate feeling to walk into a room and have so many people in awe of how much you've achieved, and still doubt yourself.

It doesn't matter how tangible your success is, impostor syndrome can plague you nonetheless. It was obvious to everyone that I had a great business, and I thought so too. It's not to be confused with insecurity. Insecurity holds you back, while impostor syndrome is the motivating force to be successful. I could grasp the concept of the company's success, but it was hard to make the correlation that I was the one responsible for that success. I had accomplished so much. Yet, to me, there were times when it seemed underwhelming. It was a never-ending cycle of continually needing more in order to feel like I'd truly merited my success.

Through the eyes of my peers, who knew me when I started at my kitchen table, I was a true success story. I went from being at *my* kitchen table to being in *their* living rooms. I'd completely changed the trajectory of my life. Regardless, I could never shake the nagging voice in my head saying, *You don't deserve this, so enjoy it now before everyone finds out.* Despite the fact that I'm fifty-three years old, these thoughts are a common occurrence. I struggle with validating my achievements, and instead I'm left constantly striving toward the next one.

Historically, women have been made to feel that they're not as capable or deserving as their male peers, or maybe that they're not as smart as everyone thinks they are. I get caught up in the idea that I got a lucky streak that just landed me where I am. Then I realize that *no,* I have been working my whole life to get here. It's a constant battle between the two competing thoughts. Often, when I'm in my pajamas in the morning, with unbrushed teeth and Chicken Little hair, I look in the mirror and I'm like, *What the fuck! How is it even possible that this is my life?* Sometimes when I'm going about my business and someone recognizes and stops me, it takes a split second to realize that they know me but I don't know them. Why would anyone want to stop *me* in the streets for a picture?

I've pulled myself up by my bootstraps and figured out how to grow a company from scratch with a product that no one had ever heard of before. I've raised a family. I've raised a mother. I've survived loss, pain, heartbreak. I've reinvented myself countless times. *Why is that not enough? When will it be enough? I think it's time that I graduate to the grown-ups' table.*

Here I was making all of my dreams come true. So you know I must have doubted myself even more when shit started to hit the fan. I was working harder than ever, constantly hustling, reinventing, designing, and always pivoting to what was going on in the market. The only unfortunate thing was that I felt I was being hindered by my business partners who held the purse strings. When I said I wanted to blow up my business, little did I know that partnering with my licensee would detonate my world as I knew it.

As I've said, when your business is on top, you never think the world is going to drop out from underneath you. You just assume everything is going to stay on track because nothing could derail you now, *right?*

With that being said, I always did feel like the rug could be pulled out from under me (PTSD from being raised by Marge Sr.), but I never thought it would happen so quickly. As it turned out, Parker Concepts and I had different core values. I never thought the partnership would result in the near demise of my team and domestic business. Bottom line, the owner of Parker Concepts didn't like that I was making more money than he was. A lot of revenue was coming in, and he thought that since he'd invested, he should make more than I did. The difference was: This was my entire livelihood, and he had a multimillion-dollar corporation. My company was his side bitch. Still, he wasn't happy when this side bitch's income was growing. I was the front person, the face of the brand and the designer. I was driving the train. My team and I were the ones who were making things happen, and he was behind the scenes. We both needed each other for our strengths, even if we weren't happy about it.

After about a year and a half of working together, the owner, Marvin, came to me point-blank and told me that he wanted to change our deal. He said he wanted to recoup his investment in a shorter time period and felt he could, since we were making so much money. He thought we should keep a certain amount of royalty revenue in the bank to pay back his investment. *That wasn't the fucking deal at all.* I didn't want to seem greedy, so I reluctantly agreed, after endless discussion. Honestly, I was intimidated. He was ruining my domestic production, and my profit margin was way down because he'd changed the pay scale. He was trying to convince me to shut down the bucket business, but that was the signature product. In order for your licensing to flourish, you need a high-end product presence to drive the brand image. He was turning everything into a real clusterfuck, and I was afraid of what else he might do to jeopardize our profits.

My licensing was growing and our cosmetic bags in particular were really taking off. The problem was that they were with another licensee, and Marvin did not like that. Although he'd never been in the cosmetic bag business, he didn't see why he couldn't be if there was money to be made . . . all by him. None of my licensees played well in the sandbox. Sharing was not their special skill. They must have skipped that in pre-K. Marvin convinced me to break up with this other licensee, a tremendously successful company with a nice team that I worked well with, and I conceded for the greater good . . . or so I thought. Bringing more products in-house did seem like the right thing to do, as we were partners. But in truth, I was still only making my royalty, and my team wound up doing more of the design and development work. We developed a line of fresh, new, exciting cosmetic bags in standout prints, mix-and-match patterns, and they were selling to tons of retailers. Marvin should have been thrilled, *right?* Well, guess what he did then? He started doing cosmetic bags with all their other brands in all of the shapes that I'd designed exclusively for him. Even some similar prints. Talk about competing in your own backyard. *I gave up a successful licensee for this shit?* If a retailer has the option of buying cosmetic bags from multiple brands, they're not going to rely on just one. In other words, the millions of dollars' worth I could have been selling them for was now majorly diluted. They were still buying millions of dollars' worth, they were just splitting it between Macbeth and the other household-name brands they licensed. All brands under the Parker umbrella. Since those brands were more established, it ate into my distribution and butchered my business potential and bottom line.

I put Parker in the cosmetic bag business, and they fucked me over big-time. Even with Walmart. I got them in the door, and then they knocked me off with their own private-label brand. Walmart should have been the last straw. To be clear, these were my business partners, the people most invested in my business besides myself, the people I expected to have my best interests at heart. I was working like a dog, while they were working against me. They would constantly take my ideas and everything I designed for them. Then they would use the designs for all of their other brands to get themselves more business. I wasn't getting a piece of that action, only they were. In typical form, I was trying to do things for the good of the whole and grow things for my brand, while they were only looking out for themselves. The problem is, it's not completely illegal. At a minimum it's very unethical; nonetheless, it really turned my stomach. It felt like a massive fuck-you. I couldn't stand back any longer and be taken advantage of while watching my brand get knocked off right in front of my eyes. When I told Parker this, they would attempt to gaslight me, telling me that I was hallucinating. In a firm where men were at the helm, it was such a pathetically classic move to paint me as the hysterical, creative, high-drama woman.

But the fact remained that I had a whole graphics team that was much more sophisticated and advanced with color than anyone on their team. Parker knew this and felt entitled to take whatever trends and visions we had. They felt that they had peed on my leg and thus owned me. We were also one of the first companies, literally twenty years ago, to come out with personality sayings. You know, things like: *Wake up and makeup* or *Too glam to give a damn.* We had these on storage pieces when I first started with Macbeth

Collection. There was no name for it at the time, so we coined the term Monoglamming. This is now a standard in the industry over the last seven years. We were way ahead of our time, and they were taking my phrases, changing one word, and putting them on their own brands, just so they could make the entire profit and not pay me. They made so much money from me, yet they were claiming that they made no money back on their investment. Let's just call it creative bookkeeping. It was really disgusting. And when I brought it to their attention, they made all sorts of excuses.

They also did other things that made me extremely uncomfortable. Their views were, at best, *very dated.* In truth they were racist and homophobic, and thought nothing about making derogatory comments in the workplace. No matter *who* was around. Their disgusting remarks made me beyond angry, and caused constant battles between us on this front. This inappropriate commentary has no place in modern society, let alone the business arena.

I'll never forget what happened with my key designer, Jennine. She's a beautiful Puerto Rican woman who was not just a member of my team but like a sister to me. We were traveling to a trade show, it was late at night, off business hours, and all the men were drinking in a hotel room with us. There was a lot of unprofessional behavior like that, which, full transparency, I was there for. We played in the lion's den way too many times. Anyway, one of my business partners said, "I don't hire Puerto Ricans; they're lazy." Jennine ran out of the room crying upon hearing this appalling remark. I yelled at him, "You're repulsive! How could you say something like that?" and chased out of the room after her.

As if I didn't have enough ammunition to want to leave Parker Concepts, this was the cherry on top of a melted sundae. I should have put an end to the partnership right then and there. It was so revolting. The previous pain, to my purse strings, I could tolerate; but causing pain to someone I loved, a valued member of my team and extended family, was unacceptable. Yet the only reason she didn't sue him for racial discrimination and a hostile work environment was because I was partners with him and she didn't want to do anything to hurt me or the future of our brand. The bottom line is that we put up with too much in the name of fear. I didn't think I could do it on my own. They were the money people. There were so many emotions and so many threats. While he was well respected in his community and a very charitable man, this didn't excuse the everyday behavior that I encountered. What was I going to do, come out and tell people what he'd done to myself and my employee? I felt like no one would believe me, so I kept my mouth shut, which was a big mistake. To this day, when I see him I get tears in my eyes. He was the first person who took a chance on me, yet he was also the first person to take advantage of me.

I would say to other women in the same position to always, always speak up; don't compromise your standards and accept the unacceptable in fear of the unknown. Know that your instincts are correct and you have to say something in the moment to put the offenders in their place immediately. If something doesn't feel right, it probably isn't; do not doubt yourself or let anyone else sway you. Though in this instance, I did say something, and I shut him right down . . . but I still remained his partner longer than I should have.

Don't ever stay too long. While everything is not a litigious moment, you have to defend yourself and those who work for you at all costs. The emotional well-being of your team is one of the most important factors in having a successful company. If everyone feels supported, the growth of the company is inevitable. Money can't be the only motivator. You can't let money rule you all the time, even if you're supporting a lot of people. You never know what twists and turns life is going to bring you.

The problem was that, back then, I didn't have the strength and experience to handle my partner the way I should have or the way I would now. There was endless fighting, disrespect, and dismissiveness. I thought about getting my attorney involved, although as soon as attorneys are entangled, things typically become messy very quickly. I didn't want an ugly scene. But at some point I couldn't avoid it, even though I always believed I couldn't afford it.

It happened when the owner, Marvin, went away to China and it was time to take our quarterly earnings. Only this time the controller was like, *No, no, not until Marvin the owner gets back and approves you taking the money*. I said, "There's no approval. In the contract, I take my money as soon as the royalty comes in. That's the deal." The thing was, they were always changing the deal to suit their best interests. The deal was whatever they said the deal was at any given moment, and I was sick of it. I wasn't going to have it anymore.

Thankfully, I'd had the balls during my time with Parker to force my name onto the bank account, so I just went to the bank and took out my portion, and that was it. When Marvin came back from China, he was furious. He said he wouldn't tolerate that behavior and he wanted to break up. He said, *It's over. We're separating.* I was like, *Fine. Fuck it, I'm over it. Goodbye. Good riddance. I don't need you.*

For many reasons, parting ways with them was going to be the right move; it was the push I needed to make the decision I should have made a long time ago. It meant that I would have to buy them back out of my business, but that I would be totally autonomous. It was terrifying and invigorating at the same time. I would finally be alone at the helm of my brand. Little did I know how out on a limb I would really be.

- Keep an eye out for red flags. Making excuses only prolongs the inevitable, and allows additional time for more damage to be done.
- Business is business; you can't take everything personally.
- The deal only works when everyone is making money.

Chapter Sixteen

SUED AND SCREWED

Thankfully, Macbeth was still thriving as I was breaking up with my business partner, but I was completely oblivious to the shitstorm that was about to hit.

My brand had always been very destination driven—we liked to call it Vacation 365—so I decided that expanding into resort clothing and beach bags was our next move. The sky was the limit.

Our resort collection was so well received. Every single hot store from Miami to Mykonos carried it. Whether you were shopping at Bloomingdale's or a beach boutique, our line was a standout, front and center. We came on the scene with a big splash. Our prints were right on the money, our shapes were classic yet modern, and our marketing showed we meant business. We were the talk of the trade shows. Clothing was a new venture for us, but we launched like a mainstay.

Life was a beach until my resort clothing licensee, Authentic Cabana, got me into deep water. They decided to make shiny beach bags using the sayings and icons that were such a signature from my Macbeth buckets. We were still making buckets at that time, so stores were even able to buy the matching buckets and beach bags, which was a unique selling point that set us apart from everyone else. Unfortunately, our licensee manufactured some bag that looked similar to the product of a company already in the market, LoloBag.

While LoloBag filed suit against Macbeth Collection, Authentic Cabana was responsible for answering the claims and settling the suit. In the licensing world, because it was the product that LoloBag was upset with, not the artwork or the licensor—aka me—I was indemnified. The important piece of this is that while my licensee, Authentic Cabana, used their counsel to settle the lawsuit, they were never actually named in the lawsuit. They pushed the public blame on me while cleaning up the financial mess. They said, *It's not a big deal. We'll cover all the costs; we know it's our responsibility.* But I should have insisted that my company name be removed from the lawsuit. Again, stupid me said, *No problem—as long as they pay, no big deal.*

LoloBag really had no grounds to sue, but that didn't stop them from wanting blood. The settlement they received from Authentic Cabana is confidential, but for clarification: Cease-and-desists are an everyday occurrence in this industry. And cease and desist is exactly what we did. In this instance, it was cheaper and quicker to stop, settle, and move on. This was a very small part of a large product line. It was nothing to make or break a brand. You would think that would have been the end of it. But that wasn't good enough. LoloBag was still pissed off. Since there was a whale icon on one of the bags, they showed it to a retailer, Vineyard Vines—whose logo is a whale—with the intent to screw us over. In my opinion, LoloBag was very vindictive and wanted to ruin us.

We had been using preppy icons since the inception of Macbeth Collection in 1999. Everything from whales and turtles to flamingos and anchors. Plenty of companies use whales on their merchandise. It shouldn't have been an issue. It was not our logo, simply an embellishment. And as I said, one of at least fifty that we offered on our line. We weren't competing with Vineyard Vines.

Vineyard Vines didn't see it that way. They sent us a cease-and-desist, which we abided by immediately. Unfortunately, the law firm that Authentic Cabana and I were using sent them an aggressive and inflammatory letter in response. I'll admit it may not have been the smoothest move. Despite our having already ceased and desisted, Vineyard Vines wasn't having it. They came at us with guns blazing, because we looked like a much bigger company than we were. In this instance, it was the artwork that was in question, so it was Macbeth Collection that was responsible, even though we didn't manufacture the product or distribute it. They were out for blood. The original letter came when I was still partners with Marvin, but in true Marvin fashion he wasn't properly insured with the correct intellectual property coverage. Conveniently, the letters sent to Marvin's office while we were still partners somehow never made it out of his inbox. After we decided to part ways, he made sure he was indemnified in the buyout agreement. Essentially, the lawsuit was initiated while we were partners, but he left me on the hook for it. I had no idea it was going to blow up like this.

I was hung out to dry, which goes to show that you always have to protect yourself, even when you think someone is trustworthy. These men looked at me as disposable, even though I was bringing them income. And when it came to liability, they didn't want anything to do with me. As long as I was making money, things were good, but once the fat hit the frying pan they ran in the other direction.

Vineyard Vines was suing me for millions of dollars. They were destroying me with discovery. Our line was so extensive, with so many prints, patterns, icons, and options, that the whale was just one of thousands of combinations offered, but every time we would go to deposition and show that we had only made $9,000 in royalties from the product over the course of many years, they would insist we were lying. The case turned very ugly, and it felt like a personal vendetta from their attorney.

After what seemed like an eternity, we wound up settling in a mediation before going to trial. I had already spent enormous sums of money on attorneys, and the settlement had to be paid in a very short period of time. I was getting annihilated financially, but a trial could have cost millions. I could have won in a trial, but at what cost? I wanted it over with.

I was hustling even harder in my business, just to keep my head above water. Licensing was still doing well, but the deficit left from legal issues and my buyout turned out to be like feeding the beast. So when a manufacturer called Posh Paws reached out to us, I was thrilled. They wanted to license Macbeth Collection for a line of pet products. Another license meant more money coming in and opportunity for more growth. Pet products was a hot category. But unbeknownst to me, the founders of Posh Paws were former employees of another licensee that I was in business with. Remember the cute tech boys from Neptune International who were killing it at Walmart? *Yeah, them.* The Posh Paws used to work for the Neptunes. When the Neptunes caught wind, all hell broke loose. Neptune didn't want me involved with their former employees Posh Paws and flat-out threatened me. They said that if I didn't turn down the deal, they would stop paying me and *skim*. For those of you not in the industry, "skim" means to trim money off the top of a partner's royalty in a way that they'll never figure out how it's missing. So basically they told me right to my face that they were going to steal from me and I couldn't do shit about it. There was one problem: I'd already signed the contract with Posh Paws.

No matter how hard I thought about this, or which angle I approached it from, there didn't seem to be a clear way out. Neptune's message was louder than ever: *You get away from those scumbags. We don't want them to know what you're doing with us and we don't want you with them.* It sounds so high school, but that was exactly the way they spoke. They were paying me so much money, and I couldn't afford to take another financial hit. So the only option was for me to personally break up with Posh Paws via text. I kindly told Posh Paws that I had to return their advance of $30,000 with a heavy heart. I couldn't work with them any longer. I had only been with them a week. No big deal, *right?*

Wrong. Note to self: Do not handle contractual issues over texts or start with the words "with a heavy heart." Posh Paws had a hemorrhage beyond belief. They weren't going to tolerate this. While optimism is one of my best qualities, it could be my legal downfall. *It's no big deal, they'll understand, what's the big issue?* Meanwhile, in camp Posh Paws, they were holding strong. They weren't going to be bullied by the Neptunes, so here I was, pigtails in the middle again. Just to clarify: They sued me *and* Neptune, all while knowing I was in the midst of the Vineyard Vines lawsuit.

Please don't forget that I had numerous employees and was on the hook for alimony to Jan, college payments for Cooper, and rent for Tori. My expenses were through the roof. I was like, *Get the gas pipe and up that life insurance.*

My attempt to fix this mess that I had somehow become entangled in was in vain. Neptune International couldn't care less that I had put myself out there and shown commitment to my relationship with them. I had not been obligated in *any* way to renege on this deal with Posh Paws. It was not in my contract—there was no legally binding document stating when Neptune had claimed ownership of me—I had done it to keep the peace and the cash flow. Big mistake. In retaliation, Neptune intentionally started decreasing the number of products they did with me and, therefore, slashed my income. I was making roughly $700,000 a year from them at one point. It dropped down to $500,000, then $400,000, $300,000, $200,000, and so on. It was ridiculous. We were doing a ton of business with Walmart, and Neptune was trying to cut me out. They were going to show me who was boss and fuck me over because as far as they were concerned, I had betrayed them for even considering working with Posh Paws. May I remind you: I had *no* idea of their history, and nor should I have. It's business, not to mention none of *my* business.

Posh Paws' lawsuit went on for years, and as a result pushed my company into bankruptcy. They sued me for millions, and in the end they won, in arbitration; they split the baby at a $650,000 settlement. I said, *No way. They had no damages; the ink was only dry a week.* I *had to* appeal. As a result, they enforced a judgment, unbeknownst to me, which froze my business bank account. I could no longer make the settlement payments to Vineyard Vines. And you thought it was messy before. The only way to unfreeze a company bank account is to file Chapter 11. It sounds like an extreme measure, but my hand was forced. It allowed me an opportunity to restructure my business and actually make payments, because my assets were unfrozen. Sidenote: I ended up paying back everyone 100 percent on the dollar, although I wasn't legally required to. This is not the norm in Chapter 11, but I felt that morally it was the right thing to do. In the end it cost me another few hundred thousand in attorney fees to unfreeze my assets. Bankruptcy is often looked at as the easy way out, this was not the case for me. After seventeen years building my business, I couldn't believe that it had come down to a pissing contest that I had gotten caught in the middle of.

Add to that the fact that Joe and I had just bought a new home together. It was the summer of 2016 when I found this amazing old Tudor with beautiful property owned and lived in by a very elderly couple with a penchant for mothballs. Now, call me crazy, but I love an old house with character, and I thought it would be a great project for us. I figured I could spend my time doing that while working on my business. I'd designed so many home products, and I'm extremely creative, so it just felt right. Not to mention that Joe's a contractor!

Well, naturally, we couldn't move in right away. For starters, there was the unbearable mothball smell, in addition to a lot of other work that needed to be done to the house and grounds. Unfortunately, this was right before Donald Trump became president, and when the election hit, everything changed. New Jersey property tax laws changed, and not in anyone's favor. Between carrying two separate properties, the lawsuits, and my bank account being frozen, all of a sudden, I'm like, *Holy shit! How am I going to afford everything? How am I going to pay my employees?* Christmas was around the corner, and there were so many moving parts. All moving against me.

The sick part was that Neptune, Parker, and Authentic Cabana were all run by men—men who happened to be really close friends with one another. They even vacationed together. Needless to say, they talked among themselves, and I'm sure some of the topics of those conversations involved me and the amount of money that I had made. They used to come to my home when I had a party and say things like, *I bought you this house.* If you bought me this house, what the hell did I buy you? My brand put many of these companies on the map; we couldn't have done it without each other. But that's the kind of people they were. They always wanted to make me feel like I owed it all to them.

When we traveled together to trade shows, we did have a good time; all bets were off and they would have us out all night. It was all fun and games until the lines were crossed. It was Friday night in Vegas at CES, and the company culture at Neptune was that Friday night was Spearmint Rhino night. For those of you not in the know, Friday is the start of Shabbat (which, in the Jewish faith, is the day of rest), and the Spearmint Rhino is a strip club (I don't think Friday nights at the strip club is rabbi approved). We accompanied our partners to the back door, because they were VIPs or incognito, you decide. Once inside we realized that they really were VIPs and were on a first-name basis with many of the employees. It was fun at first; as a non-drinker I ordered a cup of tea and complimented the girls on their smooth skin and limberness. It's always nice to be complimentary, and these girls were really good at their job. Lexi and I had to work the next day, but our partners would be off for the Sabbath, getting hot stone massages while we were busy running the show. Obviously, by 1:30 a.m. the smooth, supple girls were getting old for us. And there's only so much tea a girl can drink. We asked to leave. We were told, *See ya later, we're headed to the Champagne Room anyway*. Could you imagine? Two girls left high and dry in Las Vegas late at night by these upstanding businessmen. I guess I was one of the boys . . . until I wasn't.

If one thing went wrong, they would kick me to the curb without a second thought. I wasn't one of them at the end of the day. I felt very disposable. I trusted them, both personally and professionally, and even though I had decent contracts, they weren't as tight as they should have been. I don't jump to sue people at the drop of a hat, and I guess I didn't expect that kind of behavior from my business associates. Clearly, I was wrong, and it was a big wake-up call. The people you do business with are not necessarily your friends, even if they act like they are. I let a lot of things slide that I shouldn't have. I caved to bullies because I thought I had no other choice. From that point on, I knew that the only people I would worry about were myself and my team.

Through all these ups and downs, there was one constant I could rely on: my Super Joe. He has been my rock through it all. He did exactly what he was supposed to do: picked up the slack where he could and gave me the support I needed. He is the best partner I could have asked for. Believe me when I say that Joe is the guy you need and want when the ship is sinking.

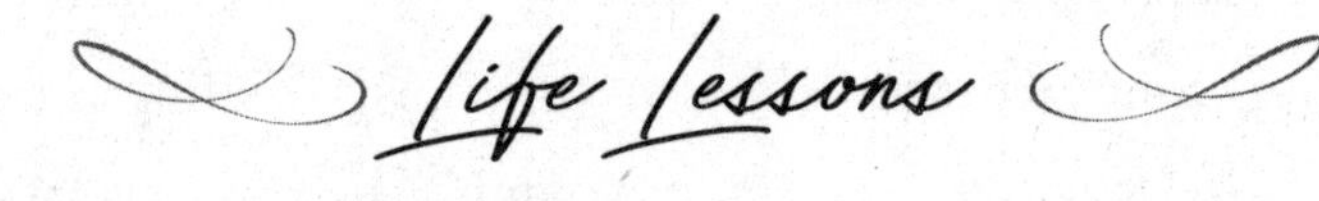

- The law is not always justice.
- Don't tolerate unprofessional behavior from the beginning; it sets a standard, and before you know it, the standard becomes the norm.

Chapter Seventeen

AUTHENTICALLY REAL

We finally moved into our new house at the beginning of 2017. It seemed like a cause for celebration, but there was *still* a lot of work to be done to make the place livable. Of course, I was also dealing with all of the business insanity; nothing was settled yet and my bank accounts were still tied up. Bankruptcy court is *not* fun. I realized at that time that I was a lot stronger than I had ever given myself credit for and could evidently weather many a storm. Randomly, who shows up on my front doorstep but my friend Jodi Goldberg, who tells me that *The Real Housewives of New Jersey* is looking for another cast member. She said, "I know you couldn't do it last time, but you should think about it. You should do it!" Maybe Jodi had a point and it was time to revisit the idea.

I'd already signed up for my own reality show with Joe that hadn't come to fruition. The kids were all out of the house. My business had taken a huge hit. And I was forty-nine years old. I thought it could be fun and something different for my career. I figured I could go on the show as my authentic self, and it would be a chance to show that all women in New Jersey aren't just Italian housewives. It was definitely a leap of faith, given the very public platform, during an extremely complicated time for me, but I threw caution to the wind in typical Marge style.

I did my little interview over FaceTime on the computer with Joe, which was a breeze. I was used to being filmed on camera. About a week later, they were like, *You're the new housewife!* It all happened within two weeks; it was such a crazy whirlwind.

I was as apprehensive as I was excited. There's no turning back once you expose your life on TV, but I had the support of all my loved ones, minus my children, who hate reality TV. They were all grown adults and I was determined to respect their privacy. It was my decision to share my life. Anyway, Marge Sr.'s and my housekeeper Marleny's enthusiasm for stardom made up for those who were hesitant. TV was where I was meant to be. The first thing that I thought was that there was no possible way it wasn't staged. Grown women do not flip tables and cause public scenes unprovoked. I had a core group of girlfriends and we'd been through a lot together, but I'd never had to dodge a flying piece of furniture.

Still, I figured it would make for a unique experience and a great platform for my brand. I had watched the first two or three seasons of *Jersey* and dipped in and out after that. Joe loved *The Real Housewives of New York*, so we were always current on that. Ramona was his favorite until he met her in person and we basically had to break her arm to take a picture with him.

Anyway, Siggy was the only cast member I actually knew; we

were just acquaintances. We lived in the same town, and while I was in my old house, she was in a rental around the corner from us. We had mutual friends, but that was it. Honestly, in my opinion she was annoying, but at the time I thought she was a good person, so when the show said I was going to come on as her friend, I was fine with it, even if we weren't close.

I thought she was going to welcome me with open arms. Unfortunately, that was not the case. No one helped me. My major *Housewives* debut was the all-cast trip to Boca. I reached out to Siggy as the newbie, and she was not at all gracious toward me. I asked her about hair and makeup for our Florida trip, and she wouldn't refer me to anyone. Funny for someone who prides herself on being the Queen of Boca. She said, *Oh, you'll find somebody yourself.* Essentially, she just wanted me to be a sidekick, and I'm not that kind of person. If anybody asks me for help, if anybody wants anything from me, I always want to include them. That's just the decent thing to do.

For example, years later when Jackie Goldschneider joined the cast, I guided her. I was very inclusive and never felt threatened. I told her to call me with anything she needed or with any questions she had. I think Siggy just did not want any part of me. It was very stressful, since I was dealing with my business bankruptcy and she kept trying to dig stuff up on me, but I had nothing to hide and had no shame. I came on right away and said, *I had an affair with the contractor, and I left my husband.* I was my authentic self. You have to be honest about everything. If someone doesn't like you for that, it's just the way it's going to be. Some people loved me and some people hated me. But eventually I turned many around.

Okay, let's do first impressions. Teresa was nothing like what I expected her to be. She was immediately warm, inviting, and felt like an old friend instantly. Melissa was very tiny in person, bubbly, and also very inviting. I was shocked that two veteran Housewives were so welcoming when Siggy, still a new girl, treated me like an enemy from the outset. Dolores and Siggy, at this point, were still surgically attached at the hip, so it was hard for me to get a real read on Dolores. I felt like she wanted to be nice, but that she was torn between me and the woman who seemed determined to be my enemy. Danielle Staub had rejoined the show that year as a "friend of," and she needed an ally, so she was seemingly sweet and attached herself to me swiftly.

I learned very quickly that *The Real Housewives* is completely real. On my first cast trip, I saw in real time how quickly things can get out of control. After a birthday cake was thrown—among other things—I went back to my room that night, called Lexi and Joe, and was like, *You can't believe what's going on here*. I think I was still in shock. I had witnessed some insanity in my life—in fact some could say that I'm accustomed to it—but this took the cake. *Literally.*

I didn't go on the show expecting to make lifelong friends, though I feel like I have. I knew I wasn't going to be braiding anyone's hair in my pajamas right off the bat. In fact, I didn't know what to expect. That was what was so appealing to me. *Real Housewives* is like a study in sociology; the complexities of the relationships between these strong women intrigued me. It is one show where women aged forty-plus are the stars, and they are encountering everyday problems and navigating them in front of an audience.

When these emotions go under the microscope and the women are held accountable for their roles in these relationships, it makes for a fascinating ride. Now I was in the passenger seat.

Listen, I'm absolutely a girl's girl. I have numerous lifelong friends from childhood. Those relationships are built on the strong foundations of love, trust, honesty, and acceptance. I do think that it reflects poorly on someone if they can't maintain friendships. One thing I cannot stand is a smoke blower. I don't operate that way; I don't blow smoke up people's asses. I'm completely transparent with everyone. I don't play games. I can tell you how I feel, you can reciprocate with your feelings, and we move on, no grudges held. Siggy wasn't used to that, and I saw right through her. She didn't appreciate that. But I wasn't going to pretend to be someone else in order for people to like me, which I think is what Siggy likes to do. That was her game. I'm confident in my own being. I don't have to hide and change myself. I'm not about secrets. I think that's why people warmed up to me right away. Siggy was trying to discredit me, and it backfired on her. So she went and did something that she *knew* would cut me to my core. She called me an anti-Semite.

Let me refresh your memory. Basically, I was trying to give Siggy an analogy. What I've since learned is that analogies don't go over very well with these girls. But back then I didn't know that. Basically, she was defending someone who was indefensible, and I was like, *Just because someone's good to you doesn't mean they're a good person.* I was trying every way possible to explain that to her and she just wasn't getting it. Her theory in life is *If you treat me well, then you must be good.* So I said something like, *Siggy, Hitler would have been good to me; that doesn't make him a good person.* The analogy insinuates that because I have light skin and light eyes, Hitler would not have targeted me. I could have said, *Osama bin Laden was good to his dog.* She just looked at me and continued on. It took her two weeks to stew over it before really coming at me. Out of nowhere, between courses of a beautiful dinner, she announced to the table, *Margaret is an anti-Semite.* Her explanation was that *You can never say Hitler to a Jew.* First of all, that's not true. My ex-husband is Jewish. My in-laws were Jewish. I did every Jewish holiday, and we were members of a temple. I raised Jewish children and was very much a part of the Jewish culture. Cooper had a Faux Mitzvah, for God's sake. For those reasons and many others, I was completely taken aback. It had been two weeks since I'd said it, and it wasn't an anti-Semitic statement. It was actually the opposite of anti-Semitism.

She thought it was going to blow up. Well, it blew up—in the exact opposite direction. People were much too smart to fall for her bullshit. The few people who did fall for it have changed their tune drastically. We all see where she is now and where I am now. The truth spoke for itself.

Regardless, at the time, I was crushed. I was a first-season Housewife with a business that had more drama than the show, and this was the last thing I needed: someone attempting to assassinate my character so publicly. It hurt to know that my family was going to hear it. Fortunately, everybody thought it was completely absurd and was so offended for me. My friends are all Jewish, my business associates are all Jewish—they were all shocked to hear such baseless accusations. I was disgusted and heartbroken that I could be accused of something so vicious. I couldn't fathom someone who could stoop so low and completely fabricate something like that. I'd never witnessed anything like that in my life.

You have to possess a tremendously strong constitution and a strong sense of self to be on a show like *Real Housewives*. People think it's all about the glamour and the money. It's not about that; it's about female empowerment, being opinionated, staying true to yourself, and being a resilient woman. If you think it's just about being famous or creating these ridiculous standoffs on the show, you will crash and burn.

A rookie mistake is trying to be one person in front of the camera when you're a different person behind the scenes. The audience can smell fake through their TV; it's called Smellavision. You can't fool people. If you act like an asshole, you look like an asshole. Context can help only so much if you fly off the handle. I am who I am—the good, the bad, and the ugly. Certain days are great and certain days aren't. Everybody's human on these shows and displays various facets of their personalities.

It's hard to be on 100 percent of the time, but that's what we sign up for. It takes acceptance to be your true self and survive reality TV. You can't always be the best version of yourself at all times. No one's life is ideal. No one's marriage is perfect. No one is without an ounce of cellulite, unless they have a little help. I don't give a shit what you say, everyone on TV has hair extensions and hairpieces. No one's hair is thick, long, and luscious on its own. Even the beautiful Italian girls with tons of hair will tell you they wear extensions. Trust me, it's not the vitamins they're touting.

Of course, I didn't know all this until I got on the show. I went on the show just thinking I was going on as myself. The first year I looked like a caricature of myself—I wore way too much makeup—and looking back now, it's kind of funny. I'd never worn such luscious and long pigtail extensions. Pigtails—more like stallion tails. Though I would never go out of the house without lipstick; that's a fact. If I had to run to the supermarket in pajamas, I would throw on a glamorous fur coat and huge oversized sunglasses. I've always maintained an element of glam, and I always love to dress up. You'll never see me with a chipped fingernail or toenail, and if anyone else has one, I'm repulsed; it could cause me to have a meltdown. But the excessive hair and eyelash extensions from season one, thankfully, I've learned to tame back.

I expected the show to be a huge commitment. It's a full-time thing. But even I wasn't prepared for just how much time is spent filming in reality. And then throw in press appearances, and the reunion on top of that. Once you're a Housewife, you're always a Housewife, until you're no longer on the show; this became clear to me immediately.

Before my first show aired, it was this weird feeling of limbo. You're holding on to your last bit of anonymity before you're announced, all while existing among swirling rumors and suspicion. I never had a personal Instagram until I started filming. I had always kept my social media focus on my brand. Then all of a sudden, my DMs were blowing up with questions about whether I was going to be the new *Jersey* wife. I didn't answer, but word was going around. I knew that I was already a good fit, but I was anxiously anticipating what the viewers' reactions to me were going to be. I mean, in my first episode I told the world that I left my husband for the contractor. I was a mixed bag of emotions.

I had a very rough year as a first-season Housewife. As if Siggy hadn't done enough, she reported me to PETA, for my husband's taxidermy bear. She denies it, but she publicly tweeted about me to them, so I knew it was her. Listen, PETA's no joke. We had to have security stationed outside my house for a while. It was emotionally draining, but I love a man in uniform, so it was okay. If anybody could take it, I could.

When the season premiere aired, we hit the ground running. I had people who loved me, I had people who hated me. People would comment on the way I looked; they'd say I needed a facelift, I had to go on a diet, change my hair, renovate my house—it went on and on. The attacks on Twitter were vicious. But then I had all the people who thought I was a breath of fresh air, that I had brought a new energy to *Jersey*. I was different. The beautiful thing was I had people reaching out to me to say that they were in unhappy marriages and asking how I'd had the strength to move on and be happy in a new marriage. They were suffering. Their children weren't talking to them. I had so many people relating to me on all levels, and that made all the hardships worth every second. I also say, *Focus on our problems, not your own*. People see themselves in each and every wife, which is what it's all about.

Did I give a shit if someone called me fat or said I needed a facelift? Not at all. Listen, I'm very confident and very secure. Show me a pretty girl and I'll show you her husband who's sick of fucking her. It's not just about looks, if you guys haven't figured that out yet.

The one funny thing was that I didn't comprehend how polarizing my pigtails would be. People were like, *Oh my God, an adult with pigtails!* I'd been wearing them for so many years that I never thought twice about it. I loved them. Jan loved them. Joe loves them. They were just *so* me. It never occurred to me that they were abnormal or shocking. All of a sudden, people had so many opinions on my hair. I mean, they were even taking polls.

The only person who'd ever said anything to me was Amy Rosenblum when she'd first told me I couldn't go on TV with pigtails and I was like, *Get out of here*. Other than that, I'd never heard it. Maybe people didn't have the balls to say something to me. *Who knows?* I thought they looked cute and I still do. Apparently, people were up in arms about pigtails, but it was completely normal to wear hair extensions down to your vagina. Of course, in the end, it was what made me recognizable. When I went out on the street, everyone could tell it was me from the back of my head. They knew right away. The first time it really hit me was when I went on *Watch What Happens Live with Andy Cohen* for the first time. People were waiting outside for me when I got there. They didn't even have tickets for the show, but they were lined up hoping to meet me.

I love that aspect of being a Housewife. I love meeting people. Everyone always says to me, *You're too nice. You trust everybody.* I'm more interested in knowing about them and what draws them to want to get to know Housewives. I'm often teased by my family and friends because I get intimately involved with people who follow the show. Late at night, I'm up answering people's questions on social media. I'm very grateful to be part of the Bravo community. If you're not good to the fans of the show and if you're not humble, it's shameful. The fans are the people who keep us on TV. If you can't appreciate that, you're in the wrong business. You have to live up to what you signed up for.

There'd been this massive adrenaline rush and all of this anxiety, and then the season was over as quickly as it had started. I was proud of the fact that I'd remained so true to myself. To this day, at the end of every season, I say to myself, *Shit, I'm exhausted. Am I really going to do this all over again?!* But after about one good night's sleep, I'm ready to go again. It's a blessing. It's heaven and hell all in one go.

Life Lesson

✦ The strongest quality you can possess is authenticity.

Chapter Eighteen

PIGTAILS ON A PLATFORM

You know what one of the best parts of being on *Housewives* is? Getting to go to the clubhouse. Being on *Watch What Happens Live with Andy Cohen*, the daddy of the franchise, is like the Holy Grail of the Housewife quest. It's what everyone looks forward to. You film your season; you ride the roller coaster; and you're rewarded with an audience with Andy. Your first time is so exciting, but at the same time the undercurrent of anxiety is like a tidal wave. You only get one time to pop your clubhouse cherry and it had been a long time since I was a virgin.

Obviously, I built my hopes up, and Andy did not disappoint—though sometimes I do worry he loves Marge Sr. more than he loves me! He got my snarky humor from day one; I mean, *I am a gay man in a woman's body*. Since my debut appearance, I've already hit double-digit visits in three seasons. I have been on with the *best* people, all funny, talented geniuses: Cheyenne Jackson, Bridget Everett (who even wore pigtails in my honor), Wendi McLendon-

Covey, Fortune Feimster, and Michael Rapaport *twice*. I've been very blessed.

Oy, I might be an overthinker, but you wouldn't believe how much thought went into my first trip to the clubhouse. Everyone knows, Andy loves a jumpsuit. So I didn't want to be a kiss ass and wear a jumpsuit, but you're also sitting from a side angle, so nobody wants a full thigh exposure. I was a little baby pork chop my first season, so I wanted to make sure I wore something that was as flattering as it was classic Marge. After much deliberation I landed on a crimson velvet tuxedo jacket over a black lace camisole and black velvet pants. The shoes were the most stressful part. The bottoms show on TV, and you don't want them too scuffed or so brand-new that you forget to take off the price tag. Most people like to wear Louboutins so you can see the red bottoms, but I opted for silver sparkle disco Guccis. I'm all about the fabulosity. If this wasn't agonizing enough, imagine trying to get Andy Cohen a gift. It's my first time in his house, and we all know The Marge doesn't show up empty-handed. Thankfully, all the stress wasn't in vain; my Jonathan Adler Chill Pill still sits proudly in its coveted place on the clubhouse shelves.

Everyone wants to know what it's like to be in the clubhouse. It's everything you imagined and more. When you arrive and ascend in the elevator, you can feel the energy level simultaneously rising. From the moment the elevator doors open and your eyes meet the glowing blue "Mazel" sign and you hear the chatter of the awaiting audience, your adrenaline goes into overdrive. I personally think it's part of the experience to get my glam done in the clubhouse.

The greenrooms are perfectly decorated in my taste, with chic wallpaper and Jonathan Adler accents. There are also always custom mini cupcakes with my smiling face printed on them waiting to greet me. Joe immediately stashes them in my bag and refuses to let anyone eat them. *Literally*, I find them months later in his office fully intact, rigamortified as a keepsake. Caroline Blanchard, the resident makeup artist, always slays my face, and of course, I use Julius Michael for my hair; he's unbeweaveable and has created so many looks that have become signature to my style. Sidenote: Jules hated my pigtails at first. He literally trashed them to my face and tried to convince me to give them up. Nothing that hadn't been said before.

It's an extremely intimate experience. Andy will pop his head into the greenroom, preshow, to catch up and give me a quick kiss on the cheek. The clubhouse crew makes you feel like family from the moment you step foot off that elevator. I know they love to see me as much as I love to see them, but I know they secretly hope that Marge Sr. is behind me with her signature chocolate babka. Don't forget, Marge Sr. is well versed in the art of the bribe. She likes to make sure to have something on hand to sweeten the deal, if her antics aren't enough to make her loved . . . which they are. Now, it wouldn't be right to talk about the clubhouse without referencing an iconic Marge Sr. moment behind the bar. She had already made some crazy statements in her previous appearances, like the time she announced that she'd had sex in a cemetery, but this one even stunned Andy. He asked her for her *Housewives* tagline, and boy did she deliver. She seductively announced that it was *I might have two cats, but I only have one pussy*. The audience erupted and Andy was left speechless. It's a rare sight to see Andy blushing. Even Michael Rapaport was impressed with her creativity.

As viewers, I'm not sure if you know, but by the time you film the reunion, you have already watched the season and have heard everything everyone had to say about you. It's time to face the music for all that shit-talking we did behind one another's backs. You see what actually happened versus what people *said* happened. You know, *Housewives* is like a bad game of telephone. But at the reunion the message comes across loud and clear, as it's delivered in person. The gowns are on, but the gloves are off, and Andy is the ultimate referee. One of the most-asked questions I get in the run-up to the reunion is *How are you feeling—are you nervous?* My answer is always the same: *No, I was born for this*. And if it comes down to a memory test, we all know I didn't have any cocktails to clog my thoughts.

The only thing I lose sleep over is our outfits. Some show up looking like they're going to a quinceañera, and others like a party rental Disney princess. I prefer to stick with classic Marge and use *Jersey* jewel tones sparingly. Listen, not everyone loves my style, but I am one of the few on the stage who are formally trained in this business. I mean, my first season I wore Pucci to my own party and I got panned! People said the form-fitting printed dress was *granny and hideous*. Now, I'm not saying it was great just because it was Pucci, I'm saying *it was great*. I was a standout in a sea of black. I mean, Pucci is iconic. Need I say more?

The morning of runion shooting, producers are calling us by

5:30 a.m. to get our asses out of bed and into the glam chair. We all have separate dressing rooms on set; it's like a bride and groom on their wedding day. We're not supposed to see one another before the ceremony. We're then individually brought out onto the stage and placed in our positions, where we'll be seated until we've battled to the death—which is nothing less than ten hours minimum. Andy then comes out and the games begin. We start off slow, with pleasantries about plastic surgeries and *So, who are you wearing?* It's not long before the formalities are far behind us. This is the chance to air all grievances. Let me rephrase that; it sounds a little too sophisticated. Basically, it's time to get down and dirty and sling some mud. The facial expressions will go down in meme history. The eye rolls, the gasps, the pouts, the tears and laughter are truly representative of the roller coaster of emotions that a reunion can be. After all, we're reliving an entire season in one day. It's like the cruelest captive therapy session that you can't escape from until you've hashed out every gory detail. Luckily, I'm a big proponent of therapy and have been practicing for most of my adult life. I've told Andy before that *This is the dysfunctional family I was meant to be born into.*

I have to mention my reunion tradition. After every one, I change out of my gown and into my sweats for the car ride home. I ask the driver to make one stop, at the McDonald's drive-through. I order a Quarter Pounder with Cheese, large fries—and a Diet Coke. I don't want to be a *total* fat ass. Simple as it sounds, it's the most satisfying reward. I'm all about the eating.

I always thought of the reunions as the Super Bowl of Housewives . . . that is, until I went to Andy's baby shower. The seating chart there was a who's who of the Housewives Hall of Fame. Every franchise, every fabulous face. I felt as if I were awaiting the birth of baby Jesus. Some brought gold, some brought diamonds, and some brought Hermès. It was such a coveted invitation that one person in particular, whose invite must have gotten "lost in the mail," just so happened to be *conveniently* around the corner in full glam. She managed to slither in. *Need I say more?*

It felt like I had gotten a bid to the best sorority on campus. The best thing about this party? No cameras were present. Just Housewives, uncut, dancing on tables with our daddy.

I do have a competitive streak. Around the time I was set to be announced as the new *Jersey* wife, the franchise was nearing 100 Housewives. There was a chance that I would become the 100th, but another was announced first. That still gets me, but hey, the 101st Housewife is still standing four seasons later. Very Cruella of me.

I always say, *Be careful what you wish for*, because the bigger you get, the farther you have to fall. While my pigtails brought the power and the party, they also brought the pitfalls. My lawsuits grew. Being on a reality show is a double-edged sword. It really is such an amazing platform, but nothing comes without a price. I think people don't realize that. Vineyard Vines sued me again, this time for $12 million, because apparently they felt like they didn't get enough the first time. After all, now I was a "TV star"—*insert eye roll here*. They thought that they could get a bigger piece of the pie. So they decided to play it all out in the public eye and try to make an example of me.

It could happen on your happiest day; that's when they want to hit you. I could be going on *Watch What Happens Live* or filming the reunion, and a press release or an article would come out headlined *Margaret Josephs Sued Again for $12 Million by Vineyard Vines!* Then you know Andy Cohen is going to ask you, *Margaret, are you really being sued for $12 million by Vineyard Vines?* And I have to say, *Yes, it's true*, while the whole world is sitting there with buckets of popcorn going, *She must be shady. She's being sued by a major company.*

Here's the reality, though: Anybody can be sued by anybody, even for baseless reasons, and you just have to pull up your big-girl panties and get on with it. You have to know how to handle tricky situations like these properly. I choose not to get super-defensive; instead I stick to the facts. I address the situation head-on. I'm honest about it, and I move forward. If you do that, you'll be yesterday's news in about two days on a reality show, because there's always some other scandal around the corner. That's one redeeming thing.

I understand why people think they really know me and my business; after all, I invite you into my life, no holds barred, every week, and I'm happy to share my story with you. There's a reason that I've always been known as TMI Marge. If I'm going through something on national television, you're there alongside me. No dirty details spared. However, people see the glamorous events, red carpet looks, and posed paparazzi shots. They don't see me squeezing into my Spanx, teasing up my weaves, and teeing up my eyelashes. Believe me, I did *not* wake up like this. It's as exhausting as it is exciting. I don't want this to come across as complaining; I am so grateful to have these incredible experiences at this point in my life. If you'd asked me at the end of 2019 how I felt about the party circuit, I might have told you that I was ready to hang up my high heels for a few months. But now, as I sit here in my kitchen in my pajamas after nine months of the pandemic, I can safely say *again*, be careful what you wish for.

Truthfully, I don't like posing for pictures for my Instagram. I love posing for pictures with people I meet, because that's more authentic. I'm not like some TV personalities who are naturally great at a photo opportunity. Like I said, I didn't even have a personal Instagram prior to being cast on *RHONJ*; I was much more of a private person back then. My team says it's like pulling teeth to get me to pose for a picture. They're constantly begging me, *You have to go get ready, you have to take a picture!* FYI, it's not fucking fun to have to have full hair and makeup on *all of the time*. So now I'm just as comfortable to go on Insta au naturel as I am all made up.

Since being on the show does demand a lot of my physical time, I've had to make a concerted effort to maintain relationships with friends. My friends date back to the beginning of time, better known as kindergarten. And it's not without work; to have good friends, you have to be a good friend in return. As a friend, I want to be a good support system, I want to be the one to answer your call when you stalk me, to drive over and pick you up off the bathroom floor when you've missed a sale at Bergdorf's. It's important to me to have a give-and-take kind of relationship.

I'd say 99 percent of my friends have been supportive on my

journey with *Housewives*. All of them say that I'm the same person on and off the screen. I haven't changed a day since kindergarten. Which is kind of scary . . . but I always was mature for my age. Friends get such a kick out of people recognizing me when we're out, screaming my iconic one-liners, like *Marge, your husband's in the pool. Say it!*

While it's definitely a novelty for my friends who can enjoy accompanying me to events, the novelty of missing out on so many special occasions has worn thin. I've missed milestone birthdays, anniversary parties, and just getting together on a regular basis. It does make me sad.

Sometimes I don't get invited at all because people assume that I won't be able to attend anyway. But it's still nice to feel included. It does hurt my heart when I'm not. To my friends' credit, when I invite them to all my parties, filmed or not, they always show up and bring their A game. They want to be there to bolster me; they donate to every charity that I'm involved with; they always come through for me. My best friend Polly in Oklahoma even opened up her home to all the *Jersey* girls. She generously had us all out to her beautiful ranch, even though, apparently, *The sunset is better in Paramus*.

My network, Bravo, truly is an incredible place to call home. They value diversity and inclusivity, and never was this more evident than in June 2019, when WorldPride marked the fiftieth anniversary of the Stonewall uprising. I have always been a huge advocate for the LGBTQ+ community and pride myself on being a strong and outspoken ally. So it was such an honor to be invited to represent *Jersey* on the Bravo Pride float. Being up there was emotional for so many reasons; it made me think about my childhood and all my mother's friends, especially Art and Dan. How far we've come from that time, and how far we still have to go. Looking out at the massive sea of rainbows surrounding the float felt like I was on the best drug high that I didn't want to wake up from. It still resonates as one of the most memorable days of my life.

I'm also so proud to be a resident of such a progressive and diverse community as my hometown of Englewood, New Jersey. We are actually only twenty minutes from the city, so it manages to feel very metropolitan, while beautifully far away at the same time. It's a melting pot of races and religions, a true extension of New York City itself. I was asked to raise the Pride flag in my town by NBC Out and my mayor, Michael Wildes, in a ceremony held in front of our public library in the center of town. In addition, I was also presented with the key to the city. As the honor was bestowed upon me, I heard that little impostor in the back of my head say, *Whoa, Marge, you're really getting the key to the city. Do you think they meant the other Margaret Josephs?* The last person to receive the key to Englewood was Rosa Parks, so I'm sure you can understand my disbelief.

This platform has provided me with some truly unbelievable experiences that allow me to work with the causes that are so important to me. For instance, I was invited to the Love Ball by Brian Kelly as his date; you may know him as The Points Guy. This party is a New York City legend; the last one was thrown by Susanne Bartsch in the eighties, and to be in attendance at such an affair was a whirlwind. I colored my hair neon pink, put on my brightest red lipstick, and squeezed my meaty ass into a couture corseted gown to prepare for the night of my life. My date didn't disappoint and neither did the evening. I was introduced to people in the industry who I had such love, admiration, and respect for. I mean, Billy Porter. His gown obviously put mine to shame.

Not only have I been able to bring awareness to and advocate for other people's charities, I have also been able to host my own charity events and highlight them on the show. My dear friend Dr. Jeff Lipton, who is the head of pediatric oncology and hematology at Cohen Children's Medical Center, has dedicated his life to treating and trying to find a cure for pediatric cancers. I was able to honor him at the Hospital Heroes charity event in my second season while bringing Brave Gowns into the homes of millions of viewers. I always felt that hospital gowns were one of the most depressing and dehumanizing aspects of the children's hospital experience. Brave Gowns are an amazing alternative to the everyday mundanity of hospital gowns. They make you feel like you're playing dress-up, and you could be anything you wanted that day of Hospital Heroes. Brave Gowns offer the children a sense of individuality during their most painful time.

And I've had a lot of insanity to endure. Between never-ending public lawsuits and physical altercations with castmates, it hasn't all been a bed of roses. Let's be honest, it's a little embarrassing to have every detail of your lawsuit plastered on Page Six for the world to weigh in on. But when you're in the public eye, this is what happens. Unfortunately, people make snap judgments, but I've been in business long enough to know that lawsuits come with the territory.

And when it comes to enduring insanity on the show, I can be a little insane too. *So* without further ado, let's discuss.

The Pool Push

Call me naïve, but I really did want Danielle to have a beautiful day and a loving marriage. I even had some of my best friends fly down to the Bahamas and attend. Her bridal suite was next door to my room, and Marty's room was directly across the hall. They only saw each other at the altar and on the plane home. Everyone knows I don't drink, but somehow my room had a tremendous alcohol bill at checkout, courtesy of the Staub family. If only that was the worst of the behavior . . .

I stood up for Marty's children and family at the wedding while Danielle disparaged them. I told her she should never get between a man and his children; her job is to bring a family together, not tear them apart. You don't demand respect, you earn it. I almost packed up my things and left. If it wasn't for Marty's family, I would have been on the next flight out. But it wasn't about me, and the wedding, truthfully, was beautiful, although not enough food for The Marge. Still, Joe and I couldn't wait to get on the plane out of there. I knew I couldn't be friends with a person like that any longer. If only exiting the island had been the last I'd see of her, but when we got home Danielle still lived around the corner from me and frequented my Starbucks daily. And yes, it *is* my Starbucks. I have lived in this town since 1991.

Being back on Jersey soil and within one mile of each other did nothing to bring us any closer. I still had a cellar full of their wine after doing them a favor by storing it, but they weren't calling us to crack open a bottle together and neither were we. In fact, we took our feud on the road and managed to ruin a perfectly good meal in Cabo with our catfighting. She threw a blow too low for me to bear—I threw a Cabernet. My aim was impeccable. Unfortunately for Danielle, her dress was no longer eligible for return. In the weeks that followed, Marty seemed geared up for revenge. Every chance he got, he gave Joe a sly dig, threw an insult, and also a drink. His aim wasn't as good as mine; no wonder he stayed in the minor leagues.

So on the night of the now famous "Pool Push," we were celebrating Jennifer and Bill Aydin's anniversary at the Taj Mahal on the highway. There were Turkish delights, belly dancers, and an abundance of roses, and everyone was dressed in red to mark this special moment. Joe and Marty were by the pool and it wasn't looking good, so I ran out there to stop the two little bulls from seeing red. When I got there in my long ruby Hervé Léger gown, it turned out that I was the red cloth to Marty's bull. Marty was spewing the same venomous insults toward me as Danielle historically did, but he made the grave error of saying them directly to my Joe's face. He was close to the edge, in more ways than one; it was literally an open invitation for him to take a dip. I mean, we *had* to cool him off. We walked away like Bonnie and Clyde, and I casually told Danielle, "Your husband's in the pool."

This is one of the funniest things about being on reality TV:

When you say something in the heat of the moment, you don't even remember it, but once it hits the screen it can become gold. This line was so off the cuff; I didn't give it a second thought. Now I've seen it on T-shirts and wineglasses, and it's my most requested line to recite. Nothing brings me more pleasure than quoting favorite lines to fans of the show, because it's how I speak every day, and the fact that someone got a good laugh from it brings me so much joy. Now, ask my family how funny they think I am . . . I think they're over me and my snide comments.

The Ponytail Pull

My wild ride with Danielle, sadly, wasn't quite over. In the weeks leading up to this next incident, things were escalating. She was spiraling on social media, which I find embarrassing on every level. Anytime a Housewife or "friend of" exhibits sloppy social media conduct, my vagina hurts. It shows a lack of control and an abundance of poor judgment. If that's what is being put out into the world, just imagine what is going on behind closed doors.

I left the house that day wearing my power pony high and tight. Danielle and I were no longer friends, and I knew I'd be seeing her at Teresa's event, but nothing stops me from a good day of shopping with my girls. From the moment I saw Danielle, it was clear she was looking for a physical fight. After her chest bumping and stepping into my personal space for an hour, I can admit that I stooped lower than I would have liked to. I had a knee-jerk reaction and poured water over her head. It felt like the fastest way to get her away from me, because I didn't want her claws in my face. Obviously, didn't work.

She snapped, sauntering over in a maniacal fashion to torch my Valentino bag and its contents in a $640 Fornasetti candle. We all stood back to let this blaze burn its course. The ponytail pull seemed like it happened in the blink of an eye, but I can tell you it wasn't instantaneous. I had time to offer to pay for the candle (I was mortified!), go to the bathroom to pee, and come back to try to clean up the wreckage of my belongings. I was bent over, doing just that, when I felt my body and neck abruptly jerk back. It took me a second to realize what was happening, and I held on to the base of my ponytail for dear life so that my hair wouldn't rip out. My body twisted as she refused to let go. All I could think was, *This is not my life.*

Even when I watch it back, to this day it still doesn't resonate that it happened to me. My loved ones watched it in horror. Even my ex-husband called me, devastated.

Making a show is one thing; this had crossed the line. But in true Margaret fashion, I fluffed my pony and put my best face forward. I knew I had to finish my season the right way. At the end of the day, this is a job and I'm a professional. I might be emotionally strong and able to compartmentalize, but physically I was left with severe whiplash that required multiple doctor's visits. I was also deeply disappointed and hurt when Teresa's part in the incident was exposed. Teresa's actions were more of a betrayal of trust to me, as we have a strong bond, or so I'd thought. From Danielle, this was expected. Teresa immediately apologized and owned the behavior, and the apology was heartfelt and heartbreaking. She still brings it up to this day as something that is so upsetting to her. I have forgiven her and we've moved on. She never wanted to do anything to hurt me. I believe her.

It's safe to say that as awful as that was, it was an iconic moment. You know what else is iconic? When Danielle's house sold in my neighborhood, they put every last thing in it up for sale. When she moved in, it had already been beautifully staged by a friend of mine. So naturally I had to take a little look around the place. I ended up leaving with an eight-by-eight-foot acrylic photograph of a horse that I had previously admired. She might have gotten my pony, but in the end, I got her stallion.

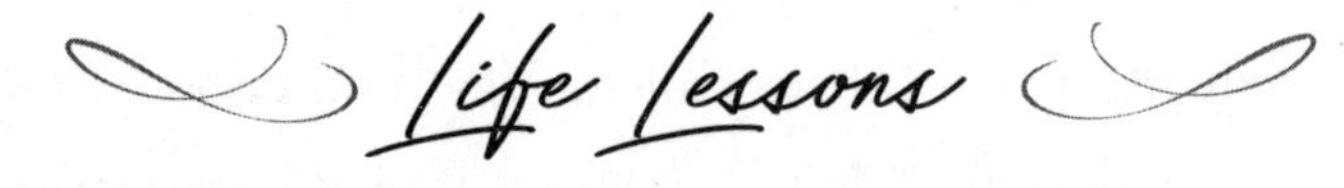

Life Lessons

- With a platform comes great responsibility. When you speak, people listen. Be cognizant of what you say.
- As important as it is to have confidence in yourself, it is more important to remain humble. The farther you go, the farther you have to fall.
- Treat *everyone* with respect. You can learn something from everyone, be it the CEO or the intern.

Chapter Nineteen

THE COMEBACK TOUR

The way I handle a setback is to see it as an opportunity for an even bigger comeback. I've been affectionately calling the last few years the Comeback Tour amongst my team. I've never looked at the negatives in my life as anything but a temporary situation. I am one to work on the solution to a problem, rather than getting bogged down in the *Woe is me*. I'm not into victims. You can brood for one day and then you have to put on your big-girl panties. I've been lucky enough that none of my issues have ever pertained to the health of my loved ones or myself. That's a different ball game.

One of my biggest big-girl-panty moments comes to mind. I was still knee-deep in the very messy lawsuit with Posh Paws, and Macbeth was in Chapter 11 and trying to reorganize. No matter how hard I hustled, this remained a roadblock, and something didn't make sense. I couldn't understand why they didn't want to settle with me. I woke up this summer morning and I said to Lexi and Joe, "I have no choice. I might have to call Posh Paws myself and put an end to this." I was hemorrhaging money in attorney's fees and I couldn't see an end in sight. And then, just like that—by some sort of divine intervention—my mother and I were out to lunch later that day at Le Club Avenue in Long Branch when I spotted one of the Posh Paws across the restaurant out of the corner of my eye. I was dumbfounded that this opportunity to face him head-on, outside of the confines of court, had landed in my lap, just hours after I had put it out into the universe. I hadn't had enough time between formulating the thought in the morning and formulating my lunch order to know what I wanted to say to him. Marge Sr. literally pushed me out of my chair, telling me, *Go over there and fix it!* There he was, sitting with his wife, completely unaware that I was about to pounce and make him gag on his California roll.

So I walked right over to their table in my high heels, with my boobs hanging out, and emotionally announced, "Isaac, I can't do this anymore. My mother's upset, I'm upset. We have to make up. It's too much." Isaac's jaw was on the ground and my boobs were at his eye level. His wife took one look at me and was like, *Do you know her? Why does her mother know you? What's going on?* Immediately, I realized what it could have looked like to an unknowing wife. After all, it wasn't my most thought-out approach, but I had to get my point across. I was like, *No, no, no! We're in a lawsuit because of Neptune!* Isaac was also clamoring to explain. He said, *It's not what you think, honey. I swear.* I was cracking up and thinking, *Oh my God, what did I do now? I'm going to get this guy in serious trouble.* Fortunately, when his wife heard Neptune, she knew the story. I continued, saying, "You have to talk to Morris; we have to turn this around." He was like, *All right, all right, call me on Monday and we'll make it work.* He just wanted me away from that table as quickly as possible, which I was perfectly fine with. Mission accomplished.

You have to be confident when you're going to throw caution to the wind like that. I knew that an opportunity had presented itself and I seized it. I went directly to the source, said fuck the lawyers, we can do this without them. It felt damn good. I called Isaac on Monday morning, and by Monday afternoon, Joe and I were in their office. We cut our own deal, made amends, and decided we were going to go into business together again. I agreed to take a reduced royalty rate so they could recoup their lawyers' fees, and I was still going to make plenty of money myself. It turns out, Posh Paws really thought that Neptune was driving the train and paying my legal bills, which is why they pushed back so hard. Quite the contrary; Neptune had not only gotten me into the lawsuit but also systematically reduced my business as a result, in my opinion. I'll never allow myself to be financially bullied again. Thankfully, my contract with them was over, and my reconciliation with Posh Paws came at the perfect time. We were partners once more and everyone was happy. As of this day, we're still making a killing together, all because I took a risk and put myself out there. Could I have picked up the phone three years earlier and saved myself a fortune and many sleepless nights? I don't know, but I know that I won't make that same mistake again.

The ups and downs of my business not only took a toll on my finances but also on my face. Every time I saw my reflection in the mirror, I was like, *When did my cute chubby cheeks drop down to my jaw?* I'd had my eyes done years prior, but my face was starting to fall. I looked like I'd been picking potatoes in the gulag for years. So I was like, *Okay, let me get a mini face-lift.* Marge Sr. had already gotten the works, a full face-lift, and she had even gotten her forehead lowered too. I thought that the mini could be enough just to refresh me.

Regrettably, the mini was a big disappointment. After a few months, it settled—and in the wrong direction: south. That was when I knew, *Call Dolores, she'll have someone on speed dial.* Turns out she did—Dr. Mark Karolak—and she loved the results. When picking a plastic surgeon, a Google search does not suffice. You have to go based on a personal recommendation. One look at Dolores's face was all I needed to be convinced of Dr. Karolak's talent. I don't like to appear filled, fluffed, and stuffed. If you rely on a ton of fillers, you start to resemble a Cabbage Patch Kid. Needless to say, I weaseled my way into his schedule with ample time to heal for the reunion. I said, "Have a heart; don't make me look at my profile on another reunion."

The bizarre thing is you actually stay awake for a full face-lift. You're sedated, but you don't go under general anesthesia. Apparently that's much better for recovery, and it was great for me because I hate going under general. It wasn't so great for Dr. Karolak because unfortunately I have a really tiny bladder and have to pee constantly. I got up off the table, with my face hanging off, three times during the procedure. They walked me to the bathroom with my IV in tow. I was banned from catching a glimpse of myself in the mirror. *Can you imagine?!* While on the table, I was also getting my eyes done *again.* It had been eight years and my lids were sagging. Dr. Karolak told me that I have an *extremely* expressive face and strong muscles, but those extra eye rolls from being on *Housewives* had expedited the process. I came out looking fantastic, fully refreshed, and healed in no time. Marge Sr. and I are from peasant stock so this really was a walk in the park for me.

While we're talking about plastic surgery, let me tell you what else was heading south: my girls. They took a one-way ticket down with no return plans. Can anyone say granny tits? They each looked like a ball in a sock. Everyone on *Jersey* has implants, which all look stunning and perky. I can never get back the hours spent taping, hoisting, and scaffolding them into every one of my outfits. Forget the bathing suits. It was time for an intervention. Cue Dolores. She had once again found another magnificent surgeon, Dr. Joseph Michaels. The only thing was, he was in Maryland. No problem; for good tits, I'll travel. He did a slight reduction and a lift, no implants for The Marge; I've got enough meat for everyone. *This* has been life-changing. Everyone thinks I look so much thinner. *Well of course I do, my boobs aren't on my stomach . . . enough said.*

Next, on to the chompers. The most surprising thing people comment on is my mouth. My whole life I was totally unaware that people felt that I had insane mouth movements. Apparently Joe knew, though. He didn't necessarily *say* anything at the time; however, he just announced, while I was reading him the first draft of the book, that he had been onto my mouth and its maniac movements for years. *Thanks for the heads-up, Joe.* Anyway, turns out, when I went to the dentist, my teeth weren't big enough for my mouth and my braces had never corrected my crossbite. Luckily for me, a very fabulous and in-demand dentist, Dr. Apa, could fix both with one simple set of upper veneers, and I'm so happy that he did. I always like to be up front about the work I've had done. It's not because I'm on TV—I've always been a vain bitch, and I say that with self-love. There's no shame in the glow-up game, and I truly believe that if you look good, you feel good. The goal should be to look like a younger version of yourself, and not like a freak.

Enough about my personal renovations and on to the other victim of the peanut gallery: my "dilapidated" house. *People, my house is 114 years old.* Rome was not built in a day. Still, people miss that memo and scream at us in the streets, *When are you going to renovate your house?!* Poor Joe. What people don't realize is that we'd moved into the house just a few weeks prior to me going on the show and had purchased the house as a restoration project. The thing with old houses is, you turn off a light in the kitchen and the AC goes on upstairs. *Nothing* was simple, but that was all right with me. An old house was my dream; you can't build character like this today.

It takes a lot of time and consideration to do a house like ours correctly. The behind-the-scenes renovations have been going on since the day we moved in. Fixing the heating isn't as gratifying to me as it is to Joe, but I guess wallpaper won't keep us warm at night. That's why I handle *The Style Guide* and he handles everything else. To clarify *The Style Guide*: When Joe and I first met he wasn't fluent in the language of The Marge. We would stand in the booth with a huge problem facing us, and I would say, *Joe, what are we going to do?* Little did Joe know, that was code for *Joe, fix it. I don't care how.* The same happened on our first trip together as I stood at the luggage carousel in Atlanta, waiting for bags that were never coming. I looked at Joe and exclaimed, *Joe, what are we going to do?* He stood there, obviously not understanding the code, and said, *I don't know, Marge.* Lexi quickly interjected with a much-needed crash course on the code: *Joe, when Marge says "we," that means you. Go handle it, and don't come back till it's done.* Lucky for me, Joe's a quick learner. Demands sound so much nicer when made as a collective. This trip was the inception of *The Style Guide*. I would handle the style, which includes clothing choices for both parties, restaurant reservations, interior design decisions, and vacation planning. Joe could handle everything else; and luckily for me, he can.

Thank God, Joe is a contractor; no one else would have been able to deal with this house. It's truly a labor of love, and we all know he doesn't let any other contractors into the house, but this time he had to cave. The funny part is, he kept it in the family. Only his most trusted guys, all named Joe and Frank, with some Dinos and Tonys sprinkled in for good measure. It's difficult for anyone to live through a renovation, but try being a contractor's wife. Most people would move out, take a rental temporarily, but that wasn't an option for us. He wanted to power on and live through it. He said, "I'm not going to commute to our house when I'm working on it every single day." I guess that makes sense . . . to him.

The other issue is, I'm not a basic bitch. My style is very unique—I call it High Hollywood meets Rock-and-Roll Lodge. That's the best way to describe it. The polite way to describe it would be vintage glamour with a contemporary twist. I like to say it looks like an old hotel where you may trip over a Rolling Stone, passed out from last night's party. The signature of my career has been working with prints, so of course it's only natural for me to wallpaper the house within an inch of its life. I'm not afraid of mixing my prints. I have a Missoni lobby that leads into a vintage jungle mural in the ballroom. We hit all the animal prints around the house. Snakes and crocodiles and leopards, *oh my!*

This has been a long-awaited renovation, and believe me when I say *no one* is more excited to see it completed than I am. I mean, I've been sleeping in my pink clothing racks for three years. People assume that it's been draining, but it really has been a passion project. Thank God for Lexi; she has been my organized project manager, because we all know I have the worst ADD. We make all of the selections together, right down to the hardware. This was my choice and I knew that it wasn't necessarily the easy one; but bottom line, I'm a fucking control freak. I make Joe nuts. The poor guy thought the pandemic might cut him some slack, but little did he know he'd be wallpapering the entire house morning, noon, and night. I knew he was capable of any of my harebrained projects from when I set my sights on a $20,000 dining room table made from a single slab of live-edge maple. I said, *Joe, I want that table*, and he said, *Fuck off, Marge*. So he made me one instead, finished with beautiful Lucite legs, that seats twelve. The funny thing is, I say I'm a control freak, but so is Joe. He is the ultimate perfectionist. When he hung the wallpaper mural in the ballroom, he couldn't stand the glaring white electrical outlets, so he took a Sharpie and meticulously drew in, freehand, the missing pieces of the design. The wall now looks seamless; I even struggle to find the outlets when I need to plug in my phone. As cheesy as it may sound, this is our forever home. Custom outlets and all.

If I spoke to my twenty-year-old self, I would say, *Don't sweat the small stuff. You have three or four more lives in front of you, at least.* As I reflect on each decade, I realize each one brought its own learning experiences and takeaways. Even standing here, I feel like I'm on the verge of another new chapter for my business and personal growth. I wasn't born into the lucky sperm club and don't begrudge those who were. I've always had big dreams, I just didn't have a name for them then. Now I call them *Caviar Dreams on a Tuna Fish Budget.* Budget doesn't necessarily mean monetary. It can represent any challenge that you face on the path toward your dreams. Now, obviously, I have faced a lot of financial challenges; you just read about them. And personal challenges? Well, I guess you're up to speed on those too. I can pull a rabbit out of a hat in a pinch, especially with Joe, Lexi, and my entire team by my side. Anything we've wanted to achieve, we put our minds to and we did. Caviar dreams became our mantra. All the lessons that I've learned on the way had to be for something, right? I've figured out a way to make things happen when they don't seem possible. Surely if I could do it, I could inspire others to do the same.

That's when I came up with the idea for an entrepreneurial podcast. I told Lexi that we could call it *Caviar Dreams, Tuna Fish Budget,* and we could empower our listeners to act on their own dreams. Each week, we bring on disruptors and innovators from all different walks of life and learn about their accomplishments. Being prosperous isn't just about being rich, it's about realizing your vision, because when you're passionate about what you do, the money follows. To me, the definition of success is waking up with a smile on your face every day and being truly happy.

So many fans have written to me throughout the years asking for business advice, relationship advice, or even just emotional support. *Marge, how did you start your business? How did you have the strength to leave an unhappy marriage? How do you manage to separate your professional and personal lives when you work out of your house? How do you build a successful team?* Now, through the podcast, I'm able to offer advice like this every week to a broad audience, while meeting and interviewing some exceptional humans.

We've had some amazing business leaders join us, including Kym Gold, the founder of True Religion Jeans; Ming Zhao of Proven Skincare; Kara Goldin, who launched Hint Water from her kitchen table; and some disruptors who burst onto the scene, changing the face of their industries, including Brian Kelly (The Points Guy) and the Oshry sisters (Claudia and Jackie of *The Morning Toast* fame), and some famous faces from your favorite shows over the years: Carson Kressley, Jay Manuel, and Patti Stanger, to name a few.

We want to continue to grow the *Caviar Dreams, Tuna Fish Budget* brand and help burgeoning moguls reach for the stars. We started the podcast at the same time that the pandemic hit. We only had three episodes, recorded in the studio with a producer, when New York and New Jersey went into lockdown. We quickly had to assume the role of producer, order ourselves some microphones, and set up a studio in the kitchen. Here I am, twenty years later, back at my kitchen table with a new idea. If the pandemic gave me one thing, it was time to reflect on my achievements and reassess my goals and skill sets. The podcast is even an inspiration to me; there's always something more to learn. Over the years, I haven't just built one brand, I've created three successful labels: Macbeth Collection by Margaret Josephs; Candie Couture by Margaret Josephs, which is like Macbeth Collection's younger sister (think Skipper to Barbie); and my namesake line, Margaret Josephs, which is a more exclusive offering of clothing and jewelry, sold through my website and select specialty stores. Each label has its own share of the market and is successful in its own right. Macbeth Collection can be found on the shelves of TJ Maxx, HomeGoods, Marshalls, Ross Stores, Burlington, Staples, Bed Bath & Beyond, and Kohl's in the form of cosmetic bags, mirrors, beauty tools and accessories, jewelry, readers, pet products, tech accessories, luggage, home office storage, home fragrance, and kitchen products. Candie Couture resides primarily at Walmart and Five Below and offers a luxury-for-less look in tech accessories and cosmetic bags and brushes. You would think we had the formula for retail success all sewn up after twenty years in the game, but no one could have seen the impact of COVID-19 coming. Almost every retailer we sold to closed its doors overnight as the wave of shutdowns affected the country. The stores that did remain open had lines out the door, but customers were waiting for toilet paper and cases of water, not printed paisley suitcases and cute cosmetic bags. This was a huge wake-up call that business had to be diverse, with many avenues of revenue stream, in order to survive this new climate. Thankfully, business has picked back up, but the landscape has totally changed. Some retailers didn't make it and have closed their doors permanently, and some of our licensees couldn't weather the storm either. Pre–COVID-19, some of my bestselling pieces were a pair of sparkly earrings that read "Party Girl" and luggage that read "Take Me Away." Now that we're all stuck at home, and the consumers' needs reflect that, it's my home accessories, pet products, and self-care items that are doing well. Like I said, a diverse portfolio of products is essential to survive in today's world. I hate using this word, but "pivot" really is the buzzword of 2020.

This has only proven that nothing is a guarantee in life. Owning real estate in New York City used to be a sure thing. Well, fast-forward to empty offices and people leaving Manhattan for the suburbs in droves. The pandemic forced people to work from home. Now, The Marge has been working from home for years and is incredibly professional in her pajamas. What I can achieve in last night's weave and lashes over homemade waffles is not to be believed. But now the world is onto me. I've always been ahead of my time.

As painful as these times are, the best ideas have been a result of the worst of times. Uber, Venmo, and Airbnb were all created as a result of the 2008 recession. If history is anything to go by and necessity is the mother of invention, we should be in for some incredible post-pandemic start-ups. The world has a lot of problems that need solving right now.

I don't care if you're two or ninety-two, it's always important to have goals; without them, what gets you out of bed in the morning? I'm not saying that everyone has to wake up with the intention of being CEO of a Fortune 500 company, but think of something you want to achieve and work toward it every day. The sense of accomplishment you will feel is priceless. I guess *Caviar Dreams, Tuna Fish Budget* is exactly the way I've always lived. Marge Sr. gave me the blueprint that life didn't have to cost a lot of money to be lived fabulously, that dreams are limitless, and opportunities are endless; you just *have* to work hard and stay humble. And if you ever get too big for your britches, call me. I'll tell you to step away from the caviar and meet me downtown for tuna on an everything bagel.

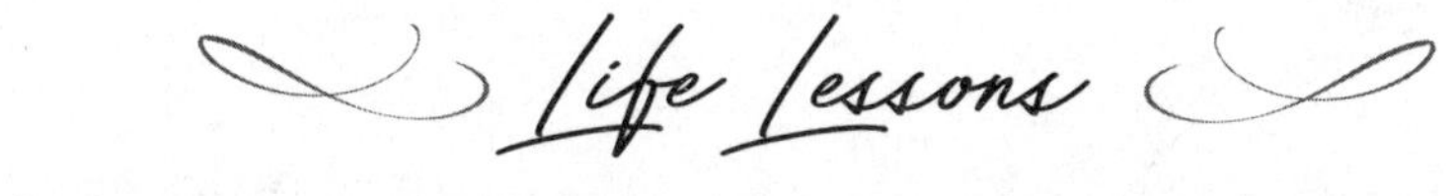

- A strong person knows when to end the battle in order to win the war.
- The most strategic thing you can do in business is diversify your streams of income. If this year has taught us anything, it's that there are *no* guarantees.

Chapter Twenty

ENCORE

Finally, at the age of fifty-three, I can honestly say that I'm exactly where I want to be in life. I wake up every day, next to Joe, with a smile on my face. Would Joe like us to be waking up to eggs on the Amalfi Coast instead of in Englewood to the sound of my cell phone ringing? *Of course*, but he knows better. It's downstairs for a quick coffee and crumb cake before the day's insanity kicks in. There are, on average, a hundred people in the house at any given time, and I wouldn't have it any other way. I've always had an open-door policy, with the understanding that you might find me pacing in my pajamas on a work call, braless.

My team is my family; there's no separation to me. We've been through so much together. I truly believe that you are nothing without the people behind you, and I couldn't share my story without acknowledging their part in it. Where can I even start with Lexi? Joe and I were there beside her in the delivery room as she gave birth to Nino. I held her left leg while wearing a cashmere sweater, as her husband, Brian, held her right leg. She gave birth like a champ; my sweater didn't even have to go to the cleaners. Joe videotaped the whole thing on his phone. It sounds kind of weird when I actually write this down for public consumption, but he's seen it all; he is a plumber, after all. Baby Nino is growing up in the office—not in a child labor kind of way but more "it takes a village." There is no Margaret Josephs without Lexi. Enough said. I also have Lindsay and Lisa, the two most fabulous, hardworking young women, who are selflessly dedicated to the cause. The cause being me. Let's face it, Lexi and I aren't getting any younger, and we've got to get the next generation in place. I have worked with Ron as part of my creative team since the beginning of my business; his design talent and taste level are impeccable. I have learned so much from him and couldn't have grown without him, though I have *never* met him in person. He lives in Oregon and refuses to get on a plane. True story. Ralph has been with me since I began licensing; he saw potential in me from our first deal and helped Macbeth evolve into a global lifestyle brand. While he has moved companies a few times in his career, he's always kept me as his constant, and he will always be mine.

I can't even get ready by myself anymore—now *that* takes a village. Marti, my makeup artist, has been with me since the Faux Mitzvah and knows my face better than I do. She's the last person I see before the important events in my life. She even creams my little cankles; she'd never let them look dry on camera. I credit my blonderexic addiction to Rafael Morales; he perfected my platinum the week after I gave birth to Cooper. I've spent twenty years in his chair, screaming, *Is it white enough?!* Although Raf can't accommodate my crazy schedules these days, he still makes sure the people I have to look at the most are blonderexic: Marge Sr. and Lexi. Julius Michael now has to suffer my incessant demands. Luckily for me, he's used to handling crazy Housewives. He's also given me a new addiction: the weave. What's a Marleny? The most energetic, overly sexualized woman at 8 a.m. that I've ever met. At any given moment you can hear her salsa-ing down the staircase, singing at the top of her lungs.

With all this insanity going on at the house, you might question how Joe doesn't jump out the window. Secretly, he loves every second of it. The girls in my office are his therapists and adopted little daughters all in one. Which is kind of weird, because I feel like they're my little sisters; but I repeat, we are not some weird sister-wife cult. Joe and I do manage to squeeze in some alone time every day. We made a promise that we would always shower together every day. Granted, sometimes it's not until 4 p.m., but we make it happen. No, it's not code for sex. It's just the one place in the house that I can't bring my phone, so we don't get interrupted.

Everyone in the house has such good energy, it's infectious, although it's not always conducive to business when we're trying to record a podcast or take an important conference call and there's a mix of Marleny's singing, Nino's screaming, and Bella's barking. We said we were successful; we didn't say we were professional.

I plan on staying on *Housewives* until I feel like I no longer belong there, or till they kick me to the curb. Whichever comes first. I love the *Jersey* franchise because it's centered on family. We've all become so involved in one another's *whole* lives. It's not like we're just meeting for a wine tasting at a vineyard; we've mourned the loss of family members together, and celebrated kids' communions and college send-offs. I may have met these women through the show, but I've made lasting friendships that I never expected. When we're old ladies, we'll be on tour together like some crazy broads, and people will say, *These women were the* Real Housewives of New Jersey, *look at them now*. But I'll tell you one thing, I'll still be blonde with big boobs.

My ex-husband, Jan, and I have come such a long way. Don't forget, I met him when I was twenty-four, so I basically grew up with him. It's hard to describe the affection I have for him, because these days it's more like he's my favorite uncle. He's seventy-three now, but truthfully, he looks like he's fifty-three. He's still hitting the gym every day, and squeezing in the parking-lot naps. He has a great girlfriend who, get this, was Joe's ex-wife's former best friend. Only in Jersey. (PS: I had nothing to do with the dissolution of that friendship.) He's my biggest cheerleader after all these years and has pulled through for me at some of my toughest times. No matter what we have gone through, we're family.

The one thing that Jan and I have always agreed on is that we have the greatest kids. Although they are all grown adults now and living all around the country, it's nice to know that we didn't fuck them up too badly. They are all successful and happy, and that's all a mother could wish for.

This kid is still close with her stepfather, Wayne. Even though Marge Sr. never officially married him, I officially gave him the title. He deserves that, and a medal for being with her. Since he moved down to Florida with my stepmother, I don't get to see them as often as I would like. They are the most loving, generous people I know, and never fail to send me a ham on Christmas.

The relationship that started it all: Marge Sr. What can I say? It's the classic case of can't live with her, can't live without her. We are so close that every emotion is exaggerated. We still fight big, but we love even bigger. I'm not sure how she got younger after all these years, but she manages to age in reverse. She could be a Hungarian vampire, I guess. I typically don't see her during daylight hours; she claims she's working, but I've never actually fact-checked that. In all seriousness, she's my best friend, my confidant, my constant. I could never imagine my life without her. I'm just hoping we don't turn into Big Margie and Little Margie à la *Grey Gardens*, though we do look good in fur and a headscarf.

So where will I be in my old age, if not Grey Gardens? Relaxing on the Italian Riviera as Signora Benigno. Remember, *we are European*.

Life Lessons

- You're only as good as your team.
- You create your own happiness.

ACKNOWLEDGMENTS

There is no blueprint to success, and every day truly is a new beginning. In writing this book, I realized the most significant lesson I have learned, which I still apply to my own life daily, is that it's not about where you started—it's about where you want to go.

I want to thank everyone who has been a part of my journey so far in making my Caviar Dream a reality. Without them, there is no me.

Without you, Marge Sr., there *literally* would be no me. Though to some our life might have seemed crazy, I wouldn't change one moment. I attribute my strength, my courage, my resilience, and my ability to outlast any broad in high heels to you. I always felt truly loved and still do. Even when you've spent our last dollar on a lipstick.

To my grandparents, the original Caviar Dreamers. You never did like tuna fish. You left Hungary after losing everything to Communism and made a life here out of nothing but hard work and love. Your sacrifices gave me the opportunity to live my own dreams and for this I'll always be grateful.

To Wayne, the only father I've ever known. The stars must have aligned when your mail route brought you to Marge Sr.

To Jan Josephs, my favorite first husband, the father of my children. We are better friends than we were a couple, but there is no question that together we are the best parents. We've been through a lot, but in the end you have always stood by me and come through for me. I am forever grateful.

To my beloved children. Being your mother is my greatest joy in life. When we met, I was a young girl, and it looked like you may have needed me more than I needed you. Now I know you all taught me more than I ever knew was possible. I love you all unconditionally. Always.

To my baby boy. You are the best parts of your father and me. We got so lucky when I squeezed you out. You are the glue, the voice of reason, and more like me than you know . . . sorry. I love you more than you'll ever know.

To Lexi, my confidant, best friend, sister, the keeper of *all* the secrets, "the real Margaret Josephs." Who knew the day that I met you, we would never again be apart. I am so blessed to get to share our dreams together. I love you beyond words.

To my amazing team. Your powerful positivity has kept us going through the toughest times, and your constant creativity has made sure the comeback really is so much stronger than the setback. Thank you for always showing up and glowing up! And a special thanks to Lisa, who lived in captivity with me to finish this book.

To my lifelong friends, you know who you are. Thank you for always sticking by me, supporting me, and keeping me grounded through our wild life together.

To my Bravo family, castmates, and crew. You put the fun in

dysfunctional. You have all brought so much color and happiness to my life. I'll never run out of stories for my grandchildren . . . and who knows, maybe a second book.

To Frances, Shari, Noah, Pamela, and all my network executives at Bravo/NBCUniversal and Sirens. Growing up with Marge Sr. was the perfect training for a reality show, and you all saw something in me that made me put that training to good use. Thank you for your constant support.

To Andy. Thank you for making me feel like I was part of the family from Day One. You are the best daddy a wife could have.

To Connor, my book agent. Thank you for believing in me and helping me put it all out there for the world to see. I couldn't have done it without you.

To Emily. Thank you for listening to me recount endless hours of craziness and making sense of it all on paper. You gave me my voice.

To Natasha Simons, my editor at Simon & Schuster, and all the fabulous team at Gallery Books. Thank you for making me a first-time author and seeing The Marge for who she really is . . . and still liking her! XX

To my sensational art director, John Vairo Jr. Thank you for going above and beyond for my cover shoot. Your creativity and vision are unparalleled. I LOVE my book cover.

To Kareem Black. Your infectious personality and insane talent made my cover shoot the most memorable and fun experience, and to say you captured the essence of The Marge is an understatement! Thank you.

To Joe, the love of my life. I couldn't have ever become the woman I am today without your unconditional love, encouragement, and devotion to all my harebrained ideas. You make me a better person and the world a better place. "Love" doesn't seem strong enough to describe the way I feel about you.